From
MAFIA PRINCESS
to LESBIAN CHIC

by

Elaine Adita Agnes

Edited by Lil Barcaski

Published by: GWN Publishing
www.GWNPublishing.com

Cover Design: Kristina Conatser

ISBN: 978-1-965971-25-3

Dedication

Ma Jaya, my Guru and spiritual mentor

Nina, my beloved wife

My Mother, who didn't have a voice to live her truth

And to all those whose voices need to be heard

TABLE OF CONTENTS

INTRODUCTION

Big bundles of money came tumbling down onto the couch from behind the mirror. My father was pulling the bills off frantically. Money was floating in the air. The mirror had always hung perfectly in place in my grandmother's home. She would have had a fit watching the scene. Earlier that evening, the rest of my family left for the airport for a trip to California. My father was supposed to be with them. Why was he here?

This very vivid memory of my father happened the summer after I graduated high school. My father and Uncle Bobby planned a sudden and unexpected vacation to California. I was surprised about this because it was a constant argument among my grandparents, my father, and my father's brother, Bobby, about where to go on vacation. My grandfather, Tony, loved to go to Florida and visited there a lot. I knew my grandmother Sue, and she would rather just stay home altogether. She loved her neighborhood and didn't like leaving her family and friends for any reason, even a nice vacation, except to go to the Jersey Shore.

Suddenly, they decided they would all go to California together, and they wanted me to go too. I was 18 and had no desire to be stuck with them for a week or more on planes and in crowded hotel rooms. I wanted the house to myself for that week. Besides that, my maternal grandfather, Lou, was my protector and he would have had a fit if I went with them. I lived with him and my grandmother, Stella, and he was not a fan of my dad or his family to say the least.

I made a plan with my best girlfriend AJ. She was coming over to have some fun (in more ways than one). We were best friends since little girls, always getting into mischief. We would sneak onto the bus to Atlantic City when we were still in grade school. We'd pack peanut butter and jelly sandwiches and go off to see her dad who worked in a big hotel down there. We took the bus from the Greyhound Terminal at Eleventh and Filbert Street. My family would think I was just at AJ's house all day, and meanwhile, we were galivanting around the shore.

So, now I thought I had the house to myself for a week and AJ and I were looking to spend some time together. We were sitting on the couch, having a cocktail made of what we could scrounge up, iced tea and scotch. Yuck! Just when we were getting into a little groove, I heard a car gunning outside our door. Suddenly, the vestibule door flung open, and my father came in. They were all supposed to be on a plane, so we thought we were living large. Suddenly, the door swung open and in comes my father.

My father always put me on guard, so I jumped at the sight of him. Great! Buzz kill. He looked at the drink in my hand. "Give me some of that, I'm thirsty," he said. He took one sip and promptly spit it out. "What the hell is in this?" he asked. "Scotch and iced tea," I said. "Jesus, if you're gonna drink, make a better drink than this," he answered and then handed me back the glass. "What the hell are you doing mixing scotch and iced tea?" "They didn't have anything in the house to mix it with," I replied. "Then drink it straight." It's not the kind of conversation you would expect from your father at 18 years old, but then again, he was always trying to get me to smoke pot with him, so that tracked.

Why wasn't he on the plane already? I was thinking. I wasn't sure if he didn't go at all or was going to join them later or what. He had a briefcase in his hand. I sat there in silence while he talked and moved around. His scent filled the room as he quickly went about his business. He always smelled good, and he was dressed in casual but sophisticated clothes—very West Coast. I loved him so much it hurt. While I admired him, I was always on guard around my father, and I hated him for the hell he put us through. I just wanted him out of the house so I could have some fun with my friend.

After a few minutes, he went over to the couch and began to pull the gold-framed mirror off the wall. My grandmother was always warning us to be careful of that mirror to make sure it wouldn't fall off the wall, so I was surprised by his actions. He began to pull those wads of cash from the back of the mirror where they had been taped to it in bundles. He lined them up and put them in his case.

The fact that there was money there was not really a shock to me. All I could think was, *get what you need and get the hell out of here.* In my maternal grandparent's house where I lived, there was always money hiding because of the Bocce club. Weekend money that was made had to be hidden until the bank opened on Monday. They might need change and would send someone to bring money home and take money back to the club as needed. So, I didn't think much about what my father was doing. The money could have been some of the counterfeit money my father printed and often got into trouble over. Maybe it was money they were trying to palm off in California while on vacation, hoping to dump it out there.

"Okay. I gotta get on the plane," he said. He kissed me and AJ on the cheek. And with that, he left. Feeling exhausted and drained from the adrenaline rush, AJ and I shut out all the lights and went upstairs. It was really nice to have her there with me and to lay quietly in her arms. I loved the smoothness of her dark Sicilian skin, curly black hair, and ethereal face. I felt safe with her.

The next morning, she had to rush back to New Jersey for work. I wished she could have stayed longer. I walked her to the front door and gave her a kiss on the cheek. I was sad as I watched AJ drive away. The neighbors were outside sitting with their early morning coffee and newspapers, and everything felt weird as if it were all moving in slow motion. I was in no way ready for what I was about to read. I caught a glimpse of the front page of the neighbor's Philadelphia Inquirer, so I picked up our newspaper and went inside. There it was, as big as could be, *CHERRY HILL CAR BLAST KILLS STAR WITNESS IN A NARCOTICS CASE*. Marty Hess, my father's one time friend, now enemy, was dead. Marty Hess had been at my house many times and now he had been murdered. I never cared for Marty. I always found him creepy but now I had to wonder if my father's appearance, the money behind the mirror, and this murder were in some connected. Marty and my father were involved in a big drug bust the year before. In my mind, I thought, *what did the money have to do with this? What did you do this time, dad?*

I felt so much fear for many reasons that I couldn't take it all in. The most wanted suspect was Louis Agnes, my dad. I wanted to scream, but I took the newspaper and tried to act calm and normal. There was no feeling calm or normal ever for me. It was a constant roller coaster ride from birth, and it hardly ever felt like I got off.

I was numb in a certain way most of my life from the start. I watched as my dad was dragged off to jail more than once, taken away. Once, my grandfather Tony had to drive him to jail with my mom and I along for the ride. I was a little girl, and I was already trying to muffle my sobs. My mom said, "Keep crying, and I will give you something to really cry about." She was flat-out crazy.

So, this was my life; Mafia princess to the Chic Lesbian topflight hair artist and entrepreneur...

and this is my story.

PART 1:

Growing Up Italian

From MAFIA PRINCESS *to* LESBIAN CHIC

CHAPTER 1

MY 8 BLOCKS

I t was six days before her 16th birthday when Mom brought me home from the hospital. I believe I was fighting with Mom in the womb, always fighting with her from when I was little. I had a past life reading and was told that indeed I was fighting her in the womb and made the decision even then that I had to do things for myself no matter what.

We lived in Mom's parent's house sharing her bedroom with her sister, my aunt Marian. Mom also had two brothers, Joe and Dom, and they shared one bedroom as well. Mom was always depressed, Dad nowhere to be found. He was only 17 himself and freewheeling.

Until I was about three years old, I assumed that I lived in Italy and that my aunt Marian was my mom. My aunts and uncles were great to me, and Marian did everything for me. She gave me a mother's love that my mom could not. She was kind, beautiful, and had a lovely voice. She would sing me lullabies and read me books, not my mother. Mom was out there fantasizing about my dad. Depressed all the time.

My first three years were very nice for me. Then along came Uncle Orfie (Orlando), Aunt Marian's boyfriend. I learned that they were going to get married and move across the street. I was inconsolable. That Christmas, I lost it on my Aunt Marian. Kicking and screaming, I threw a tantrum because she was leaving me.

They got married and the wedding was absolutely beautiful. My aunt looked like Snow White, and the wedding was fit for a queen. I was in the wedding, and to this day, her wedding book is one of the most beautiful I have ever seen. They moved across the street, and I saw her most days. They were both so good to me. They took me all kinds of places, bought me crinoline dresses and all my underwear. I showed baby pics to Philly friends later in life, and they said, "Now we get it. This is why you are still a princess."

I was about three when I began to realize that my world was bigger and that I was not, in fact, in Italy. In the eight blocks surrounding my house were three sets of great grandparents, all from Italy and two sets of grandparents. My grandfather Lou's brothers and sisters were much younger than he was, and they also lived in that eight-block radius. Grandfather's dad came to America first, leaving him and his mom behind until he could send for them. Later they had American-born children, but he was at least ten years older than his siblings and was more like a father figure to them than a big brother. We would visit their houses, and all their kids were cousins to me too. Mom would walk me up and down the neighborhood, and we would visit everyone almost every day.

The Bocce club that my grandfather ran was only two blocks away. People were always at the house. My grandfather was very social and well-liked, so the house was always filled with Italians and Italian food. I only had Chinese take-out food as a reward or to make up to me if he had punished me.

So, I can see why I thought I lived in Italy until I was sent to nursery school. *Wait a minute—this is America,* I realized. I was sent to attend nursery school five blocks from the house with my cousin Sammy, who was just days apart from me in age. It was a public school and most of the kids were Italian but with a few Irish and

Black kids as well. However, the teacher spoke only English. I always felt safe when I looked around the room to see my cousin Sammy was there. His presence made me feel safe. Later in life, I told him how much that meant to me. "How could I have helped you," was his response. "What was I gonna do? I was so little too." All I know is that I just felt like, if he was there, everything was okay. Until school, I had never been away from my family. Now I knew I was in America, but in my whole life I have never said I am an American. I'm an Italian and that's that.

Tonics to Make Me Eat

My mom didn't feed me properly. She would leave me in my crib sitting, and she was daydreaming while I went hungry. My aunts and uncles would come over and scream at her. "Why are you not feeding the baby?" My grandfather would go ballistic that I was not fed. He would have his mother, Concetta, who lived around the corner, come over to the house and make this Italian concoction with whiskey or rum, honey, and a raw egg, and whisk it up and hold my nose and make me drink it. It was supposed to make me gain weight and be healthy, which it did but it also probably made me a little drunk! I was the smallest of the kids, and he wanted to make sure I would grow properly. My grandfather thought I was going to die so he took me to Dr. Bartone to see what he could do. He gave me tonics to improve my appetite. Unfortunately, it did a great job I and I began to gain weight. My problem with my eating disorder began from the time I was a little girl. One of my aunts chided me in my 20s—"Tonics still working on you, huh?"

From that point on, I started getting chubby. I don't think it was the tonic. I think it was many things like all the craziness. I was already learning to stuff my tears. My father would take me when he was out of jail to a lot of different places. I was hoping and wishing for him to love on me but that didn't happen. He would take me down to *The Lakes*. It's a place everybody would go in Philly. I thought we were going to have a really nice time. He took a blanket, and I thought we were going to go there and sit by the water or walk around. And then he did his number...he would sit me on the blanket, cozy up to me, and grab my stomach and say, "No one's ever going to love you if you're fat." I had also started biting my nails. Who wouldn't bite their nails with all that trauma going on around me all the time, right? Then he would take one of my hands in his and say, "Look at those hands. They look like little truck driver hands." This is what my father would say to me. Remember that I only saw him a few times a year. That left a mark on me for the rest of my life, and I believed him. I was looking for love. You know that expression, looking for love in all the wrong places? Mine was in food and in pleasing people. I know those are common things that a lot of people experience. My cheerful and funny personality led to making people laugh all the time but inside I was hurting. I never felt I could tell anyone my true feelings. I didn't even have words for my emotions. They were all bottled up inside.

I knew I could find love all within my eight blocks. There were at least fifty of us, including three sets of great grandparents. I could stop in at my aunts' houses. I knew who made cavatelli on Sundays. I knew who made the raviolis on Saturday. I loved Aunt Mary, who lived a block away and made the best Italian cookies. So, I knew where to go because my mom took me around to visit family most days from the time I was a baby. She would say, "Let's go see Aunt Marian across the street or my other aunts' houses, and I knew they loved me because when you visited them, they fed you. To Italians, food is love and love is being fed. That set a precedent for my whole life, a precedent until later in life when I switched this behavior of seeking love with the food.

The Italian Market

The Italian market and its surroundings were the heart of our city, and the church was its soul. It was and remains a big part of my heart and soul. It's hard to contextualize because the experience was amazing. It started from the 1100 block, so 9th Street, along where Pat's Steaks and Geno's was, and it went all the way through past Sarcone's Bakery. It started to wind down around 9th and Fitzwater.

There were restaurants and other great bakeries in that area; one that belonged to my good friend Donna's family. Sometimes I would stay over in their apartment that was on top of the bakery, and the aromas of the breads and Sicilian pizza would waft up the staircase. Up the side streets and all around were little cafes. Back in the 1950s and 60s, until the health department put a stop to it, a few of the butcher shops would have hanging portions of dead animals, pheasants, or pig heads. It was both scary and gross to me.

The streets were lined with stores and in the street and sidewalk were stands with all the best vegetables in season. When shopping in the market, you were not allowed to touch any of the fruit or vegetables. The proprietors packed it for you, so it was great when they knew your family. Still, to this day, my mouth waters at the thought of Jersey tomatoes. In the stores were spice shops, bakeries, Italian cookies, and candies. And, of course, several stores that made fresh pasta and raviolis—anything you could dream of. The market was central to the neighborhood and within eight blocks of our house, the Bocce Club, St. Mary Magdalen grade school, and church. There were restaurants and bars along the way that served roast beef and pork sandwiches and other Italian delicacies.

Ninety percent of the owners and workers were Italian. There were gorgeous men and boys, eye candy even to a growing girl, working behind those stalls. We went every Saturday. Encompassed in that area was and is my favorite, Claudio's Cheese Market. My grandfather knew the owners of a lot of the stores and stalls. But as far as cheeses go, Claudio's was it. Whenever I am home now, I'll go straight there. They make their mozzarella fresh every day, and they have a lemon ricotta that by itself tastes like cheese pie. The store is amazing and carries provolone, all the different olives, fresh anchovies, pasta from Italy, some of the best olive oil, and burrata. In the market, there was also *Ralph's Italian Restaurant,* which was always great.

The best part for me was going with my Grandmother Stella. It was her day off from working at a distillery, and we went every Saturday together. I loved her so much, and she was as sweet as could be. I loved when we walked there, and she would hold my hand. It was hard because the place was packed like New Year's Eve in New York. My grandfather's friend, who played cards at our house, had a big corner space and we could bring all our bags there from the other stores, so we didn't have to trudge around all down the streets carrying them. And then Uncle Joe would come get the bags in his car.

Sometimes, during the week, Lefty Lou would hand my mom $100 and send her over to Claudio's to get some cheese, olives, and maybe a little soppressata. That was when the father and brothers owned it. Now, the son owns it. Meanwhile, we had a cold cellar in the back of the basement where we hung cheeses and soppressata and my grandfather's brandied cherries and his strung-up Calabrian peppers. My grandfather's nephews and family from Italy would send care packages one or two times a year. My grandfather Lou would send money every month or quarter to his family that he thought was so poor. My grandfather was like that, always giving to those he thought had so much less. When my grandmother and grandfather's sisters went to visit them in Italy, I didn't want to go. But they came back with stories about the nephew's marble floors and beautiful home they had. They told him to stop sending money. Every few years, the uncles came to visit. I already didn't like them. They were mean to my grandfather when he was little. My grandfather used to tell me the story of when he was a little boy waiting three years in Italy to come to America. He and his mother Concetta were living with the family. Two of his uncles used to torture him by hanging him from an olive tree over a steep drop. They were mean to him in other ways, and I believe that was the root of some of my grandfather's anxiety and depression. So, when those same uncles came to the house and the rest of the family were making a big fuss over them, I wanted no part of it. I could sense their meanness in their faces and all I wanted to do was protect my grandfather. My Grandfather Lou brought his Italian culture to our home, and most of the other Italians did their best to do the same.

As I got older, I went by myself or with friends and would run into lots of people and by then knew some of the gorgeous guys. Even 60 years later, when my mom died, I went to 9th Street and ran into old school friends who offered condolences for my mom.

One time, when my wife and I went back to Philly, I went with her friend to go pick up some food from Ralph's and of course cheeses. We ran into one of the guys I went to school with who owned Ralph's. The restaurant was closed, and he was going in to cook. He was so sweet and let us in and sold us containers of stuff. Nina's friend went back and told her she had never seen me so happy. That was my little Italy.

Princess and the Puppy

I remember it was just a usual summer morning and I was in the living room in our house. I heard a little commotion on our front steps and wanted to go see. With my grandmother and mom right behind me, I opened the door and there was this very tiny, cute puppy on the front step. "Oh my God! A little puppy!" I shouted while jumping all around. I was so excited, and the dog wanted to come in our vestibule but looked a little scared. So, I went to pick the puppy up from the top step and as I looked to the side, I saw my Pop-Pop Lou with a big smile on his face. Holding the squirming puppy in my arms, I was in awe. My mom and grandmother were standing behind me, and my grandfather came up and told me that the puppy was for me. "She's mine!" I was so happy and delighted, and the endearing look from my grandfather and the love between us was so beautiful. His being so happy that I was happy meant more than getting this beautiful gift. I loved my Pop-Pop even more than my adorable puppy. I named her Princess, and she brought us all so much joy and happiness.

Francine the Queer

My mom's Aunt Louisa and cousin Phyliss lived just a few blocks away. My mom would walk me over there, and they would have their babies in baby carriages. We would stroll around the neighborhood together. I might have been four by then, and one day as we passed the ice cream store, I began to beg. "Ice cream, ice cream, Mama. I want ice cream." In those days, the pharmacy would often have an ice cream counter in it. My mother gave in to my begging. "Okay, Okay!"

At the counter in there, I saw a person sitting on a stool and he looked to be half man, half woman. He was wearing makeup and was odd to me. When we got outside, I said, "Mom, that person is half man and half woman." "Shut up," she hissed at me. Phyliss began laughing. "That's just Francine the queer in there." He was a big guy though, and he was often dressed as a drag queen for the Mummers Parade held in Philly in New Year's Day. He did business with my father and my Uncle Bobby as it turned out. He installed carpet or something. His appearance didn't bother me at all. Actually, I was intrigued none of that ever bothered me. But I did hear that he knifed someone which was concerning. I later learned people would make fun of him, and he would get violent, which I understood. One day, I saw Francine driving in his convertible with his boyfriends. I pulled my brother Louis away from the street so fast I scared him. His cute little face was so innocent. I just didn't want him to be seen by Francine. I heard from other people that Francine the Queer liked young boys, so I wanted to keep my brother away from him. I didn't know they meant young boys like guys in their twenties, not kids.

Aunt Connie, Uncle Fred, and Cousin Russell

My mom's oldest sister, Connie, and her husband, my Uncle Fred, were bright lights in my family. She was brilliant and went to Temple University and had a scholarship to medical school at that time. She would tell me all about her life when we were together, and I could listen to her tell her stories over and over, especially how she met Uncle Fred. He went to Wharton Business School and was from India. They were both going to the International House at the University of Penn for dances parties and socialization. Her best friend, Helen, used to go with her. Of course, my grandfather wanted Aunt Connie to marry this Italian guy from South Philly. My aunt was not having any of it. So, Helen, her best friend, told her, I think I have a guy for you. Uncle Fred was like a knight in shining white armor. He was six foot two with jet black hair and always reminded me of a cross between the actors Omar Sharif and Clark Gable. He was Persian but when the Ayatollah took over Iran, his ancestors walked over to India. His family was from a higher caste system, and they had servants and money. He was also taught by the Jesuits. My aunt was a beautiful, petite, Italian girl with the most soulful and brilliant eyes.

They were married by the time I came along, and Aunt Connie always wanted to have the first-born grandchild. I didn't know that till much later. Well, guess who came along first? Yup, me! My cousin Russell was born six months later, so at least she had the first grandson. One time, my aunt confessed that she was very angry at my mother and jealous of me. Imagine that from a woman who had anything and everything that she wanted in life. She wanted Russell to be the apple of my grandparents' eyes, but I got there first. I think my mother was in some sort of competition with my Aunt Connie because Connie was my Grandfather's Golden Child.

For a very long time, Russ and I were bonded at the hip, because no matter where they moved, my mom, who was only 18, would take me with her to babysit Russell while Uncle Fred and my aunt were both working. And I loved that, because a big part of the time was in New York or North Jersey, which was right next to New York City. Uncle Fred, at the time, was a buyer for Gimbels in New York. I loved the city, the stores, and the big Thanksgiving Day parade. Gimbels in Philly ran their own Thanksgiving Day parade until the 1980s. So, even as a very young child, I was very aware of how much I liked all that pomp and circumstance.

Russ and I were like brother and sister until our siblings came along. By that point, my Aunt Connie and Uncle Fred were back in the suburbs of Philly, and my aunt gave these lavish parties for family and friends. My Uncle Fred's family came from India one time, and oh boy, did I love those beautiful men and women with their saris and painted toes with bejeweled sandals. Here I was, maybe at seven at that time, and I was teaching them to do the twist.

I always loved being the center of attention in a good way, and I especially loved to dance. I learned so much culturally and intellectually from being around my aunt and uncle. It was totally different than being in South Philly. My Uncle Fred was refined and powerful and I never heard him yell, curse, or scream. He never had to raise his voice when he meant business. Russell was so mischievous, but very quiet, and he was always getting punished like me.

My cousin Russell and I didn't see each other as much and our paths changed when we turned 13. When he was in grade school, Russell was able to study German and other things that I had never heard about or had a chance to learn about. I didn't realize how jealous I was until I got into high school, because then all I did was take languages. I wanted to show I was as smart as he was. But at the age of 13, our lives started to change. I was getting chubbier, and he was very slim. He was very active playing tennis and riding his bike. They had the Country Club where they lived, and they would go all the time in the summer. I was not into any of that, although my aunt offered to take me to the club anytime they went. I was more into my city friends at that point and my cousins. I just wanted to hang with my Philly cousins. I only wanted to be in the city, living the city life. I was not cut out to be a suburbanite ever. Russell and I would hang out around holidays though.

I loved going to my Aunt Connie's, even if Russell wasn't there, because they had over an acre of land. I used to love to go help her around the house. I loved to go there just to talk to her because she would give me great advice, and she would tell me about herself. I was and still am a South Philly girl through and through, but I loved the aspects of what she taught me. That's what really helped me get to where I am. She would correct my language. She would correct how I spoke, even how I chewed gum. She was just different from the rest of my family. In many ways, she was more like my grandmother Stella's family in *Conshohocken, PA*. They were a little more upper-class Italians. I loved sitting at the table and being a part of the Mazda family. My Aunt Connie and Uncle Fred were brilliant. My aunt shined much more than my uncle. I don't ever think she got a chance to use her true brilliance. My uncle did not want both of them to have big careers. They thought feminism was the ruination of our country. Bullshit. I find women much more powerful and just as smart, if not smarter than men. I always wanted to have more knowledge, because knowledge is power. And every human should have it and be able to share it.

When I start dating Paul, Russell and I came back together again because he had a girlfriend, and I had a boyfriend, so we doubled dated. Then, when he married Mary Pat, we bonded and became very close again. I loved his wife, she was beautiful and intelligent, and when I got married, my wife also adored her. To this day, Russell and I are still very close, and he comes often to Atlanta to visit and flies me around in his plane. We are as close as when we were kids.

No Longer the Only Child

I was three when my mom got pregnant again. I remember my grandfather screaming all the time. "How could you do this again? Can't you stay away from that man?" Things like that. He was furious that my mom and dad did this again. They were still not married. They got pregnant with me when they were barely in high school. Now they had done it again. I think my mom was more addicted to my dad than in love with him. She was too young to really understand love anyway, and she had no safeguards to keep her from getting pregnant, so she kept having kids with him. And he was a great con artist when he wanted something.

I was four when my brother Louis was born. In my memory, my parents were married by then. Grandpop Lou, Mom's dad, had my dad's aunt drive them to Maryland where you could get married quickly. "I never wanted to get married," my father told me when I was older. He was forced into it and acted like he was somehow a victim. Bullshit!

The women had a baby shower for Mom at my dad's parent's house. I learned later, when older, that during the shower, my dad went to my mom's parents' house, where we were living at the time, and robbed it. My grandfather kept silver coins stored in an old workman's chest. My dad knew this, so he went there while everyone was at work or at the shower and stole the money and some jewelry. People didn't want to tell me those stories while he was alive because they knew I would confront him.

When mom brought Louis home from the hospital, I fell in love with him. He was the chubbiest of us, weighing in at 10 and a half pounds. My mom got toxemia with him, but he was so cute, and now I had a new playmate. He was really smart and an incredible artist. Of course, my dad was hardly around, and my mom's parents and siblings picked up the slack.

My grandfather Lou was unaware of how much he hurt my brother with his comments. He went on forever about how my father never bought Louis a pair of shoes or anything, not even an Easter suit or a communion suit. My grandfather Lou was very hurt and angry that my father's parents didn't help much. My grandfather Tony was extremely frugal with his money. They all came out of the Great Depression! There were always huge gaps between the grandfathers. Tony was a construction worker and made a good salary. He liked having a new car and going on a vacation for a week down to the Jersey Shore or Florida. My grandfather Lou was the opposite. He owned the bocce club and had three different positions there, one of them being a bartender. So, his money was more fluid, and Grandfather Lou was ridiculously generous with his money, as much as Tony was frugal.

My brother Louis was really sweet and as he got older, the pain of my father's absence really bothered him. All his besties' fathers were around, especially his friend Anthony. Anthony's dad was sweet and generous, especially with his time, and took Louis out with Anthony and me and his daughter. To this day, I am so grateful for all my friends' dads who treated us just like their own children. When Louis was about 10, he won a contest selling subscriptions for the Philadelphia Inquirer, and he a bunch of other boys went to Spain.

I'm not sure how old he was when he started drinking wine in the park with the other boys, but he would start crying when he drank, so one of his friends would come and take him home. He and I were wired the same way when drinking wine. I couldn't drink or I would either start acting wild or cry as well. When he cried, his emotions came out about my dad. I forget what age his bestie moved away, but I know how he felt. He felt lost. I could see it in him. The besties of our siblings were family as well and growing up in such proximity to our grade school and church, a lot of us were bonded and looked out for each other and our siblings.

A lot of kids start using pot early on, including my brother. Louis got injured at Willow Grove Park on a ride on the Alps and so did some of his buddies. He got a payout from the insurance company. I felt like that was a set up for a few things including later on his drug addiction. Life was hard on those Philly streets. I felt so sad for Louis, and I was already carrying the weight of the world on me. My mom slept a lot for a variety of reasons, or she was just in a daydream about my dad all the time. I couldn't tell her anything about my brother's drinking or anything my brother was doing, lest she hit me. She would say I was lying and causing trouble. I did not want to tell my grandparents either. Well, guess who I had to ask to step in, my uncle Joe. My uncle Joe went to work around seven o'clock to play his music at wherever he was working, and he couldn't really control Louis and Sadie. He really tried hard.

A year after Louis was born, my mom got pregnant again. I was five when my sister, Sadie, was born. She was beautiful but far more fair-haired and tinier. I loved her and treated her like my little doll. Her tiny body couldn't handle all the craziness and stress, and she had a lot of stomach pains. So, my grandmother Stella gave her paregoric, and it seemed to calm her. But who wouldn't have a nervous stomach coming home to all the family screaming? And once again, Great-grandmother Concetta and my grandfather's sisters and everyone else were always telling my mom what to do. And then there was me. Because my mom spent so much time in the bedroom, and once again, my father wasn't around that much, I became like a little parent. And of course, I always wanted to run the show, even at such a young age. I loved my sister, and everyone else did, too. I'm sure my Uncle Joe was tired of my mom having babies since because of it he really lost a lot of his teenage years. He was 19 at that point and still lived at home until he was 31 years old. My siblings never listened to his punishments anyhow. My uncle by then had regular gigs every night and weekends and girlfriends so he wasn't around as much. I liked when he was home because things didn't get so out of control. It really was like he was the sanest and he used humor a lot to make us laugh.

One of my fondest memories of my sister and I—and there were many—was when she was about 7 years old, and my mother allowed me to take her on the bus to Center City about two miles from home to the Lit Brothers Christmas Village. It was on Market Street and was beautiful. I was so excited to take her there, and I had money to buy us treats and hot chocolate. And then there was a big snowstorm, and we had to wait a long time to go on the number 47 bus to take us two blocks home. I was so worried about if she was warm enough, but she was bundled in this snowsuit that made her look like a little Eskimo.

We finally got home, and there were delicious bowls of soup waiting for us. It was a wonderful bonding experience, and we still talk about it today. I was already hyper vigilant because of all the drama around us and my pedophile father. He had already started sexualizing her from pretty young. My father's lawyer at the time was Bobby Simone and on weekends he would have great pool parties. I knew he didn't want to take me, and I didn't want to go. I'd rather stay home with Susie Q and my grandfather, Tony. Sadie looked adorable, and she had on a new bikini. He did give my grandmother money when he wanted us to be dressed a certain way.

Sadie's sensibilities were right on, and she started crying when he picked her up in his arms. She wanted to stay home with me and my grandparents, but I kept saying, "he's your father, Sadie." I was trying to calm her. I look back now, and I just want to vomit. I knew he wanted to flaunt her in front of his friends. I felt like he didn't want to take me because I was chubby by that point. And his saying, "Nobody's gonna love you if you are fat!" all the time! So, in my head, I was like "Fuck you, I didn't want to go anyway." But I do remember not even being asked to go.

I remember Grandmom Sue saying, "Your dad's going to take Sadie to a cookout at Bobby's, and you are gonna stay with me." I knew in my head why, and it really did hurt me. But he did so much mean stuff to me, and I had already started to build the walls around my heart and the shame he kept putting on me. As a child, this mix of fear, confusion, and shame all bottled up inside was overwhelming.

The Italian Holidays

I have so many fond memories of growing up. Christmas and Easter were my favorite holidays, when everyone piled into my grandparents' house. Christmas was so amazing. My grandparents and their five children and all of us kids would be together. Christmas Eve was always about the Feast of the Seven Fishes, and everyone would pile in this tiny house on Marshall Street with gift boxes and lots of love. There would be Christmas music on, and everyone would be singing. Uncle Joe and Aunt Marian had the most beautiful voices of all. My aunts and uncles, who lived in the suburbs, started to head back after the singing. But then my grandfather's brother would come over with his wife. It was so funny because they both sang, not so good, and they were very juiced up. We loved them, but it was like, "Oh my God, please don't sing." My Italian great grandmother could not accept that her youngest son married an Irish girl and stayed mad about this until she died. She had forbidden him to marry her, but he did anyway, and she told him to never bring her to her house. But they would come to our house. Of all people, this Irish aunt wanted to sing "Ave Maria" and by the time she attempted this, she'd already had a good amount to drink, and it was, let's just say, funny! I loved that aunt because she always spoke up for my mom, and she was right on. I was very surprised she was able to get away with that much before they shut her up. Even so, we were all having a great time, so we just sat there and listened and behaved. Now, my uncle Joe's wife was a professionally trained singer with a strong, powerful voice, and she could sing "Ave Maria," like nobody's business.

Later, after most people left, the big card game got started and went on till the next morning till at least 4 or 5 a.m. When we were little toddlers, we had to go to bed early and wait for Santa Claus, and the other people had to go home with their kids. On Christmas Day, it started all over again. Everyone came back around one or two o'clock and we were all excited to be together again. Christmas Day was another big day with meatballs, sausage, pork gravy, ravioli, sometimes lasagna, we were big on pasta, and we always had fennel on the table and a big salad, lots of Italian bread, and always homemade wine. Then a little later, of course, the ham and some accoutrements would come out. And then the best part, dessert, was Italian homemade cookies and cakes and always a tray of Cannoli, Baba Rum pastries, and *Sfogliatella*—shaped like clam shells—and there were always fruit and cheese trays on the table.

More singing, more playing of cards, more, more, more of everything. The festivities went on for the whole week, with everybody stopping by, exchanging gifts, eating, and talking, and lots of laughter rang though the house.

Then came New Year's Eve with a smaller version of the Seven Fishes dinner. And then New Year's Day with the roast pork, roast beef, macaroni salad, potato salad, and all the Italian delicacies. So, these were the holidays, and they were fabulous. We were all so happy. Easter was similar. No matter what the other courses were, there was always the meat, gravy, and raviolis, and then ham, macaroni salad, and shrimp…on and on.

And then on one of my favorite holidays, Easter, my grandmother Stella and I would bake all day on Good Friday. She would make the beautiful Easter braided breads with the colored eggs and sprinkles on them, the Italian Easter meat pies, Pizza Rustico, the rice and ricotta pies. She would make about 30 of those braided breads for all the families to take home. The best part of Good Friday was that my grandfather was at the Bocce club, and when it closed from noon to 3pm, while everybody was doing the Stations of the Cross, he came home. He had to be quiet while we baked and that was hard for him because he always had to tell my grandmother and us what to do. When we were baking, she wasn't having that. I guess they really loved each other, although I rarely ever saw them kissing. He was always affectionate to her, but she would push him away because she was very embarrassed by his displays of affection, especially if he had too much to drink.

Italian Easter Meat Pie
Also known as Pizza Rustica or Pizzagaina

INGREDIENTS

For the shell:
- 2 lb. flour
- 3 eggs
- ¼ cup Crisco
- ½ stick margarine (soft)
- ½ cup sugar
- 2 T pure vanilla extract
- ¼ t salt
- Warm water
- Egg wash to brush the top

For the filling:
- 2 lb. hot Italian sausage
- 1 lb. sweet Italian sausage
- ½ lb. capocollo
- ½ lb. boiled ham, cut into ¼ in. cubes
- ½ lb. Genoa salami
- 1 large stick of pepperoni, diced into ¼n in. cubes
- 12 eggs
- 3 lb. ricotta cheese
- ½ cup Pecorino romano, freshly grated

DIRECTIONS

Make the shell. Mix and knead together all ingredients with a little warm water to make the dough. Divide the dough. Roll out enough dough to cover the bottom of your 9"x13" baking pan. Spread dough over pan. Keep remaining dough for top covering or checkerboard topping.

Make the filling. Cut up and fry all meats together and drain well. Mix eggs and ricotta and romano together in a large bowl. Then stir into meat mixture and mix well.

Assemble. Pour filling into prepared shell. Cover with strips of dough in a checkerboard pattern. Brush egg wash over top of dough. Bake uncovered at 350 degrees for one hour. Check to see if any oil from meat comes up. If so, blot with a paper towel and keep baking until golden brown. Let the pie cool for 15-20 minutes before serving.

From MAFIA PRINCESS *to* LESBIAN CHIC

CHAPTER 2

THE SECOND WARD BOCCE CLUB

A t the Bocce club, my Grandfather Lou had two business partners who started the club with him. It was my grandfather's whole life. He came over from Italy at eight years old with his mother once his father had settled in America and was able to send for them. As an Italian immigrant, he made sure he had a job and got educated. He had beautiful penmanship and spoke perfect English. He became a forest ranger. That's how he met my grandmother, Stella. He was working up in Conshohocken and was going around on a horse.

King of Prussia in Conshohocken was an area that was all farms and families. My grandmother Stella's father had a big house there and Lou rented a room from him in their home. So, that's how he met my grandmother, and they start seeing each other in secret. They wanted to get married, but her father wasn't having it. He disowned her because he felt like my grandfather was lower class. He came from a poor, Italian family and Stella's family had more money. They ran away and married anyway. He loved his wife, my grandmother, Stella. They settled in South Philly and my grandfather finally opened the Bocce Club known as the *Second Ward Bocce Club* which was a block and a half from our house, right on Sixth and Washington Avenue.

It became the epicenter of our life. Everything was about the bocce club. He went there almost every day. He and Combare Pete bought it, and the members paid a membership fee. Everything was there. There was a restaurant in the club and some famous chefs came out of there. A whole lot of activities went on there. My grandfather's name is Lou, but he was also called Lefty. They called him Lefty because he played with his left hand and was a champion Bocce Ball player.

In Italy, the bocce clubs, and playing bocce in general, is set up for just men to participate. Women never played bocce unless it was a family event. It was where the men could go and meet like their private club. They would drink, talk about women, and even bring the ladies they had on the side there.

We weren't really allowed to go to the Bocce club. My grandmother, Stella, hardly ever went. Sometimes if they had big parties or holiday events, she would go then but not as a regular thing. The mafia hung there, the detectives hung there, and the girlfriends hung there, probably throw in a few prostitutes, too. I don't know if other people's wives went, but my grandmother certainly didn't. Later on, down the line, my Aunt Connie blamed the fact of my grandfather's cheating on my grandmother because she didn't get all dressed up and put make up and sexy clothes on like the women at the club. She didn't hang around the Bocce Club like the other wives, so she wasn't there to keep an eye on him.

On my grandmother's death bed, I told my other aunts about what Connie had said. They went crazy and were screaming so much that one of the nurses called the social worker. They said the woman he was cheating with wasn't even pretty at all. My grandfather's four sisters adored my grandmother Stella and said she was a saint, and she really was. My grandmother was raised on a farm and was soft spoken and demure. She wasn't like the outspoken and loud Mallace side of the family.

So, in this neighborhood of mine, I was given a strong sense of the Italian culture. They had Christmas parties at Club for the families. People would get dressed up and someone would get dressed up in a Santa Claus suit and we would all line up to get gifts from Santa! It brought jobs to the community. It was a big slice of Italy in America, a slice of home to many of them. There were hundreds of people that joined. I know this because I used to help my grandfather write out his postcards to the members reminding them of the monthly meeting. They would come to business meetings once a month to talk about the Bocce Club's agenda.

My grandfather was a United States Champion at bocce. He had many, many trophies, and he was featured at the Balch Institute. Up until then, I didn't know how famous he was, but they had all his trophies displayed there and *The Philadelphia Inquirer* interviewed him. He never told any of us. He was just a very humble person. I only discovered all of this because they were having an event at the Balch Institute when I was living in Center City. I went to see these two Italian female filmmakers who were speaking and showing excerpts of their films. When I walked in, I was shocked to see all these pictures and his trophies there. *That's my grandfather.* I knew his trophies. They were big, and then there were all these pictures of him and this newspaper article that they had done two weeks before. He never told any of us in the family.

The Bocce club kept my grandfather employed. It paid our bills. He paid for everything for us because my father never paid a penny, of course. My grandfather paid for us to go to parochial school, and he built the club from the ground up. It was a beautiful building. It was humongous, taking up two square blocks, and sat on the corner. There were two huge bars, one in the front and one in the back. The bars were made of hand-carved wood and were gorgeous. They had local musicians playing on the weekends, including my Uncle Joe and his band. That's where they had parties. There was a little street that ran from the Bocce club almost all the way down the street to my great grandmother's house where my grandfather grew up.

My mom would pick me up from grade school, and we would go by the Bocce club. And so, I would beg her, "Please, please take me to see Grandpa." She always had this look on her face that said, *If I don't take her, she's not going to shut the hell up.* All my life, I would ask my mother things, and she would just look at me like that. And then, of course, responding to that look, I would say, "Mommy, please, please. I want to go see Grandpa," and as usual, I was very animated. She would tell me what a pain the ass I was, but I would always win. There were days she must have pre-made arrangements. She would say, "Okay! We'll stop in," because she knew he didn't want us in there when there were a lot of men around. She didn't have a chance anyway. I would just skip up the steps to the club.

One thing to note, my mother did not like the side street we would walk up to get to the club. She didn't like that street because she was scared of the people who lived there, but not me. I would argue with her about it, even then. The poor, Black people on that block never caused any problems or bothered anyone in the neighborhood and we lived in harmony. They had a lot of respect for my grandfather because he said good morning to them all the time and treated them with respect, whoever was sitting out there, and he would give them stuff. And I, of course, emulated my grandfather by saying hello to them when I walked up the street. I learned and extracted so much from every moment spent with my grandfather.

I did have a little fear, but I pushed past that fear, and I would say hello to the people on that block as we passed just like he did. I admit that I was always attracted to Black people even from very young. We would go down the shore to Atlantic City, and we would go on the rides on the Million Dollar Pier. There was a young Black kid and another kid, a white boy, who my girlfriends and I would have a ball with. I had a crush on the light-skinned Black boy who worked at one of the gaming stands where you filled a water balloon and the first one to burst a balloon won a prize. In fact, I always had crushes on people of color at one point or another.

My grandfather Lefty was the kingpin of his Bocce club. A real boss. And me? I was the princess. He'd sit me high up on a stool, and I'd feel like I owned the joint. Very few patrons were there when I was there. Just me, him, and my mom and the clink of the bar glasses he wiped down while keeping an eye on me like I was something precious. Like a little treasure. That's how it felt. He gave me treats and gave me either Coca Cola, which was special, because we didn't drink soda at home unless it was a special occasion, or he would make me a Shirley Temple which was super special. Then he would hand me money to put into the jukebox, and money to get peanuts or chickpeas from the little machines with the knobs you turn to release a handful.

I would call the club fabulous with a masculine feel. The club was so well-built—all brick on the outside and clearly the work of Italian artisans. The bocce alley ran the length of the small street behind the building. It was made for men, for hanging out, playing cards, talking. The place was slow after lunch until the evening, with maybe a couple of old-timers playing cards, but nothing much happened. At night, that's when the real action started. And Lefty—he ruled it all. He was my grandfather, but in that world, he was something more. Not mafia at all but connected enough that you knew not to cross him. He made it clear without ever saying a word. I knew he had the contacts to make things disappear, including my dad. But that was not my grandfather! I used to wonder sometimes why he didn't.

My grandfather built a small empire. The bocce club fed so many people, and in return, my grandfather took care of and fed so many people. He was so well-loved by the community and had a big heart. There was a homeless man, Carmen, from the neighborhood that my grandfather took in. He kept him clothed and fed and hired him to run cash to or from the house as needed on the weekends when the banks were closed. My grandmother kept the cash in the freezer. I guess that's cold hard cash. Once when the power went out one summer, my mom put everything from the freezer into the slop can, unfortunately, including the cash. My mother could do no wrong even when she tried. Well, until my grandfather needed his change and realized about $3,000 was gone.

But I was his little princess. He'd let me go all around in the Bocce alley, into the different rooms, and the really beautiful bar where he put music on so I could dance. And when my grandfather saw me, he was so happy. Even with that, I still grew up feeling so insecure. I think it was because I felt like the sin my mother and father made; the product of sex not sanctified. He was my protector and kept me away from my father as much as he could. While I felt safe with him, I later realized that he was keeping a lot from me, and that at his hands, I was suffering from my mom's mistakes and his criticism of her.

During the time of my growing up, Angelo B was the head of the mafia. He lived next door to one of my best friends, and he was known as the gentle Don. He was sent from New York to run the Philadelphia mob. He took with him a guy from the New York mob that had actually betrayed him. The New York mob asked Angelo what he wanted to do with this guy that betrayed him, how they should handle him, how did Angelo want him to kill him? Angelo B said, "I want him to be my lieutenant. Have him come with me to Philly, and he has to remain loyal."

Angelo never really scared me, although I kept my distance. Some people fawned over him. I had a certain amount of respect for who he was. I saw him at some family functions, but it really wasn't a big deal to me like it was to others. I grew up with the mob, and there was always this combination of fear and respect. I knew their kids and hung out with them. Even though the papers said my dad was an associate of Angelo B., he was not a made man because he was too headstrong and independent. I'm just like my father in that way. But my father hated the mob because they didn't want drugs in the city.

My father...my father was a whole other kind of monster. I always knew the kind of power my grandfather Lou had. My grandfather knew all the same people my father knew because of the bocce club. My grandfather probably could've had my father whacked any time he wanted. Hell, sometimes I wished he had. But he never did. Maybe because it was his son-in law was the father of his three grandchildren. But most of all, because that was not who my grandfather was. My grandfather was not a killer. I could see it in his eyes. He had soft, kind, beautiful golden-brown eyes that were very romantic and warm, and there was never any hate in them. What he could have done and what he did were two different things. Even though he had a big mouth, and he hollered a lot, especially if he was drunk, he had a sweet side that often came out.

One night, all the men from the club were playing cards at our house. They used to come home from the Bocce club because it closed at a certain time when they legally had to stop serving alcohol. So, they would come to our very small house where you could hear everything everyone was saying from one room to the other. My uncle and grandfather were talking one evening and I heard my grandfather say, "Not even the army wants him," meaning my father. That left me feeling very insecure like my dad wasn't good or smart enough for the military. Later, when I was older, I reflected back to that conversation and I thought, *did my grandfather mean the army, like the real army, or the other kind of army?* We never said the word Mafia in our house, but I came to know the euphemism for it was "army."

Jersey Boys...or Philly Boys, Who Knows?

The Jersey Shore back then was my happy place. A lot of my family and friends' families went there. While the details are murky, I remember this one summer being there with my dad and mom and grandparents was a big deal. One day, my father told me he was going to take me to the Town Tavern in Atlantic City, because he had a meeting. Town Tavern was one of the best places to go for Italian food. All I really wanted to do was go on the Boardwalk rides or the beach, but okay, food before that sounded good! As we walked into the restaurant, we got the grand hello. As I learned later in life, my father had some money or some kind of partnerships in a few restaurants in Philly, Jersey, and Vegas. I never really knew what, but I didn't ask any questions. I knew better and I didn't care to know about his so-called business deals at that age.

As we walked to the table, he told the host that he needed a little table for me. We went into the dining room, and there was this very long table with some incredibly handsome, Italian guys. They were much younger than my grandfather's friends that I knew from the Bocce club. He introduced me and explained why I was with him and that he was getting me some pizza. Yay! My dad shook all their hands and greeted some with the Italian kiss.

As we approached the table, I felt this strange feeling of power and fear. Some of these guys were formidable. I didn't know any of them and to this day couldn't tell you who was there. I remember wishing that Lee was there because he always made me laugh. I can still feel the fear of how powerful and scary some of the guys were. I never knew what to do with those strong feelings. I have realized over the years that I had the ability to focus on the good and let go of some of the other stuff. The gems that I took away and used in my business dealings are that I was used to being around intimidating men, whether it was with my father, grandfather, or others. This so helped me climb the ladder of success in my career and served me well in my life, as you will later see.

Lee Katz, My Jewish Uncle

Sometimes my dad would have his friends over for dinner or drinks. I was about eight when Lee came along. From the beginning, I felt safe with him in a way that I never felt with my dad. I loved when he and my dad would tell stories and get me going. He was one of the few friends of my dad that I never feared. Even when my dad went away, Lee always came by. He was like a funny uncle, who always made me laugh.

One of my favorite stories that I loved was the time that he and my dad went to some bar for food and drinks and these guys were in there busting on them. Lee was pretty drunk from what they told me, and these guys didn't know what they were in for. Lee was a boxing champion and he and my dad started to beat the crap out of these guys. The guys fled the restaurant and that was that. I realize now that my whole life I was looking for my heroes and who could protect me. I found that in Lee!

Lee made me feel like a princess (maybe a Jewish princess) early on. He drove me around in his brand-new convertible Cadillac. He always seemed to have a new car. Lee had a dog named Whiskey, who was some kind of collie mix with fluffy, long hair. I loved Whiskey, but my grandmother did not like all that hair around the house.

Lee was a Jewish prince whose family owned nursing homes and his father was a judge. I didn't have a clue about any of that at first. I just knew that when my dad was away, Lee would come and pick up me and my Grandmother Suzie Q and take us to his penthouse in Atlantic City. His parents also had a family home in Margate. I got used to that lifestyle really quick. That was the beginning of being treated like a princess and getting used to the finer things in life.

From an early age, Suzie Q, my father, and grandfather Tony took me out to a lot of nice restaurants. And so did my mom and her sisters and their husbands. And I was taught etiquette. My Uncle Joe called me a spoiled brat, but I wasn't one. I think he was just jealous. So, I always felt secure in my going out to eat and of course my father taught me the fine art of dining, flirting, and handing out the big tips. Those were all the niceties and advantages I had about learning how to be in the world!

Lee was a constant in my life and that felt good! When I was 13, my father convinced Lee to take me to his uncle, a well-known doctor, for diet pills and to put me on a diet. My father thought that would help because I loved Lee that much and I'm sure Susie Q had her say in it. My father was always concerning himself with getting me to lose weight. My weight became a whole family issue. Sure, I loved food, but I was also trying to protect myself from my father and other nasty men!!! As the years went by, Lee became more endearing to me, but my father had his own interests in it. Like I have said before, I've had his number from the age of two. What he really wanted was for me or my sister to marry Lee because he was so wealthy. That was how my father's mind worked. It wasn't going to be me, of course, because I was fat. That's not at all what I wanted anyway.

I think that's why my dad told me when I came out that he always knew I was gay. That is also totally not true. I have had several intimate relationships with men, including my 16-year relationship with Paul. Even to this day, I am attracted to gorgeous, handsome, well-dressed men and over the years have dated a few.

Lee eventually became a state representative. He worked in City Hall. His father was a judge who, I was told, was the person responsible for dismissing my father's legal case so he didn't have to pay fucking child support. We all helped Lee get elected. I even helped by doing phone calling and campaigning.

There was a big businessman named Brouse whose construction company built things like office buildings with restaurants and stores in them, but there was a law that you couldn't build a building taller than the hat of William Penn on the famous statue of him in City Hall. Brouse asked Lee if he would be able to do something to change that law so he could build his twin towers. As stated in the newspapers, Lee told him, "Yes, but I have to talk to somebody about it." Lee went back to Brouse and said he could get the law changed if Brouse would pay what he called something like a "taxing fee," meaning a kickback of 10 percent of the entire intact from the twin tower. Brouse said he would meet Lee to discuss final arrangements but went in wearing a wire. Brouse had ratted Lee and his co-conspirators out to the Feds.

Lee lost his job as state representative and would wind up in jail for 10 years for this. He probably told my father what he was up to because they were still buddies, but I didn't know if Dad was part of this scheme. I remained friendly with Lee. When he got out of jail, he went back to his hometown where he became the mayor. When interviewed about it, the townspeople said they didn't care about his "mistake." They loved him and they were loyal to him, something that is common amongst Philly people. When we love you, we forgive and forget!

From MAFIA PRINCESS *to* LESBIAN CHIC

CHAPTER 3

MY ITALIAN PRISON

My Uncle Joe would punish me and make me stay home. One time he punished me for the whole summer, and I was not allowed out of the house. I discovered the book *Gone with the Wind.* I read it four or five times that one summer, and I wanted to be like Scarlett O'Hara. Her story blew me away. That book was one of the first adult books I ever read. I think I came into the world with that same temperament and bravado. I knew even that when I was young, in my mother's womb, that every step along the way, I would find a way to do something positive, something to change my world. I wanted to be like Scarlett and follow her life motto, "After all, tomorrow is another day!"

No matter what I tried to do, my family members would criticize me. I liked to draw, and my grandmother would say, "Stop wasting paper and pencils." My mom bought me day glow paint and it would shine when the lights were out and glow in the dark very psychedelic. I used it to paint the walls in the basement and boy, that didn't go over well! By the time they realized I had done it, it was too late. I was very artistic as a child, but no one encouraged me. In fact, they would be angry at me when I wanted art supplies or was creative. My mom did buy me some things like Mary Quant crayon sticks for eye shadow and cheeks, but I wanted to put blue streaks in my hair. I used the sticks to color strands of my hair. I guess I was ahead of my time on that one. All of those kinds of things got me in trouble, especially in Catholic school. They were always met with negative comments from many of the family members, especially two of my uncles. They really didn't see the artist in me, and I was continually being tapped down.

My Uncle Joe became my warden, and my grandfather disenfranchised my mother. No matter what she said or did, one of the members of the family had something negative to say about it. They shut her down so much, that she basically gave up.

Mom's Time at Wanamaker's

My mom worked in South Philly for her first job or two. My uncles opened a salon for Mom and another aunt, hoping my Aunt Marian would also go to work there. It was not in a great neighborhood. Mom had already gone to cosmetology school, at an Italian-owned and operated place that offered excellent training. I would go visit my mom at school, and I would see what she was doing. It was very exciting to me. And then my mom got her first job. My uncle Fred was the VP at the furniture department at John Wanamaker's Department Store. He got her a job there, but she had to start at one of the make-up counters as her first position. She wanted to get a job as a hairdresser there, but those positions were sought-after, so she had to wait. Wanamaker's was the primo department store in Center City, Philly back in the day. People came from all over to see the beautiful tree that was three floors tall, covered in lights, with the music synchronized. It really was amazing. The store was famous for years and recently it was bought out again. They are now using it in a different way with small shops on each floor as a multi-use building.

On the first floor was the makeup department. There were all these beautiful makeup counters and when I was around 12 or 13, I was allowed to go visit my mom on my own. I walked into Wannamaker's one afternoon, and they were filming this makeup and cosmetic line by Lydia O'Leary, that was used for pigmentation, for scars and to help with damaged skin. I saw this presentation as they were filming it, and I was just so impressed. The reason I mention this story is because there were two things I always wanted to do since I was a teenager. I wanted to either have a makeup line or I wanted to have a gourmet healthy food line kind of like a Weight Watchers. I realized many years later that both of those ambitions led to helping people. I really went into my businesses wanting to help people even with cosmetics, hair, and makeup.

So, I loved going into the department store. I loved looking at all the makeup counters where they sold lines like Estee Lauder, Givenchy, and all that. I would watch the salesgirls do presentations, and my mom worked at one of the counters, so from the time I was a young girl, I never had to use crap makeup. Nothing like Bonnie Bell, that's for sure. I had Clinique and Estee Lauder and all the high-end products. My mom would bring this stuff home because the girls in her department got samples all the time. She would buy her makeup for herself at a discount, so I was always in her makeup bag.

One of the times my mom was called to do makeup, there was a famous guy there named Mr. George Masters, and he needed someone to work with him that day. It turned out that he was Marilyn Monroe's makeup artist and hairdresser, and he was presenting in Philadelphia. This affected me in my career for many reasons. He asked my mom if she wanted to go to New York and work with him. When my mom was young, she looked like a toss-up between Marilyn Monroe and Madonna. She was hot, but she truly was beautiful, and she was sensuous. That stuck in my mind my whole life and sparked my imagination. From then on, I got it in my head that I would someday go to New York to work. However, every time I went to New York to get a job, I realized they were a different level of artists in New York. It was a stark contract to what I was used to in the types of hairdressers I was working with in Philadelphia. These people were famous and phenomenal.

At my younger age, I was too insecure to believe I could match up to them. I had basically learned hairdressing from my mom and Aunt Marian. My aunt had a salon in her home, and I went there most days after school. I wanted to help and learn. When my mom came home from work, she would go to my aunt's house and they would practice on each other, doing color and all the new stuff like foils. My mom would teach Marian, and I was learning as well. My mom went platinum blonde, and she looked fabulous and glamorous. I believe I was jealous of her because back then as a child I could never get thin like her. I loved how she knew how to change colors from a slightly champagne pink, platinum, or an icy lavender just with different rinses. I fell in love with color, and it became my own specialty over the years. My mother finally got to cut and color hair in the fancy salon inside Wanamaker's. She was an all-around stylist, an expert at hair, hair coloring and cutting, and make-up. In fact, she was one of the best make-up artists I have ever known. You had to wait to get into the hair salon, because spots in good hair salons like that are usually filled, and it was well worth the wait.

My mom's career, where she worked, the salons and all of that, ignited my passion for what I wanted to do with my own life. Eventually, I worked in a downtown South Philly salon too, but I didn't like it. I knew I wanted things to be better for myself, and I stayed on that path. I wanted to be around the international crowd.

Cops on the Doorstep

One Sunday, when I was about four years old, I was spending the weekend with my grandparents, Tony and Sue. They were in the kitchen making the Sunday gravy for our dinner, and I was sitting with Dad playing games. Even then, somehow, I knew he was a pedophile. Though I didn't have a name for it, I knew it my whole life. He never molested me, but I had this feeling about the way he looked and behaved around young people. I am a very sensitive intuitive Pisces and just know things. I get these feelings about people. It's an interesting gift to have, but a good one if you pay attention to it. I always felt wary around Dad.

Even so, I sat quietly with him and played. I was looking out the window when I saw cop hats coming up the porch steps, one cap, two, three. My father looked up just as they were getting to the door and came rushing in the house. He went running out the back door from the kitchen and jumped over the fence. The police ran after him in pursuit.

I sat there stunned. My grandmother began to cry, and my grandfather was yelling. Somehow, I more or less checked out emotionally. I kept waiting for him to return for dinner, but they had caught him and taken him to jail. That was a shock in and of itself. They took me back to the Mallace grandparents where we lived. My maternal grandparents fed me, which was something my grandfather did often as one of the ways he soothed me.

This kind of thing was why my mom's parents hated when I went to my paternal grandparents' house, even for the day. I think the real beginning of my food addiction started here. I wasn't chubby before this. This was way before we talked about PTSD, but I learned a lot about it later in life.

Kidnapping

I also remember being about four years old, and my mom and dad were fighting. We were at Dad's parents', and they weren't home. Mom started throwing dishes and cups at him, and I was really scared. So, I ran into my dad's arms. He left my mom screaming and crying at home. My dad put me in the car and said we were going to go see his Uncle Bill and Aunt Marie. They lived in Langhorne near a very famous ice cream store, Greenwood Dairies. I remember him parking the car in this weird space between trees and not in the driveway. I loved seeing Uncle Bill and Aunt Marie. Bill was my grandmother Sue's brother. We all loved them.

It was a fun day with my dad. I remember him putting me on the top of the fridge and I had one of my little crinoline dresses on and he was letting me jump into his arms, the crinoline part of my dress floating up as I jumped. I think my dress was yellow. I began getting tired and was allowed to take a nap, not waking up until the morning. I overheard them talking about the cops looking for my dad because my mom and her parents had alerted the police that he had kidnapped me. So, that fear was invoked in me. As much fun as I was having with my aunt and uncle doting on me, I wanted to go home to my mom. Uncle Bill called Sue and told them we were there and something about me falling asleep and we stayed over. The search was called off, and my dad took me back home to Philly. I believe that may have been the beginning of me tracking where I was because from that day on, I was afraid he would always take me from my mom and everyone I loved.

Later around that time, I remember sitting in the back of my grandfather's car taking my dad and dropping him off at gates. My mom was holding in her tears, and I began sobbing. Of course, she says to me, "If you don't stop crying, I will give you something to cry about."

Catholic School Prison

All the kids in my neighborhood went to school at St. Mary Magdalene DePazzi Parish. It was the first Italian parish in the country. It was all Italian! You weren't allowed in if you were Irish or German or anything, unless one of the parents was married to an Italian. That's the only way in and there were very few of them. One kid got in because his father was captain of the police force. Shit like that is what it took to get in if you weren't a full-blooded Italian!

So, I had to go to Catholic school. I hated every fucking minute of it. The only thing I enjoyed was walking to and from school. And the other thing about me was I always had a posse in school, and we would all walk together. I had them with me all through my life.

I was always a handful in school. I loved making people laugh and wanted to entertain them. In kindergarten, the nun said to me, "If you don't keep quiet, I'm going to put you on the boys' side." I thought, *Oh, great. There's Raymond, there's Joe, they're all my friends, so put me there.* And she did put me on the boys' side. It didn't bother me. That followed me all through school. When I was in high school, my mom had to come to see the principal like a million times. I remember my history professor saying, "If you don't keep quiet, you're going to go to detention." And what did I do? I said something!

In first grade, I was dealing with all this stuff at home. The nuns gave me Ds on my report card partly because I missed mass at our church and for my attitude. You had to go and sit with your class every Sunday at the nine o'clock mass. But I was dealing with trying to get to my other grandparents on weekends. I did not get bad grades on the main subject matters. I was very smart, but no one ever told me how smart I was or complimented me other than my Aunt Connie and Grandmother Sue who encouraged me a lot. The nuns had no idea what I was dealing with at home. The nuns were worried about me getting the envelope for church. And my grandfather did not want me to go over to my other grandparents. And it was push and pull. My mother would get my little clothes ready to go to my other grandparents and my grandfather would come home and start a fight. He wouldn't let me go. So, I never knew where I was going to be on weekends, and that was very painful for me; it was very hard on me. And then having the nuns take it out on me for not attending church with my class just made it all the harder. Sometimes, if I did get to go to my other grandparents', even though it was only a mile away, they would have to take me to the nine o'clock mass. I had to be there at 8:30 to line up with my group.

The other reason for getting bad grades was, of course, for lack of self-control and my undiagnosed ADHD that followed me all through school. I acted out a lot because I really didn't want to be there. I wanted to be home where all the fun and entertainment was happening. But I did get a kick out of being the class clown, making the other students laugh and always getting in trouble. My Aunt Connie, my mother's oldest sister, was right on the money. She said I should have been going to acting school and become an entertainer. But maybe it's good that I didn't become an entertainer with all the craziness that goes on with them.

I did like some of the nuns. I loved Sister Cosmos. She made me want to be a nun but that changed right away. In second grade, I had Mrs. Pagano, and she was a tight-ass teacher, but she was great. She really enforced discipline. That did help me a lot.

My uncle's band used to practice in our living room when I was a kid. I would love to dance to the music even at five. I would rather stay home from school and dance along in the living room than listen to the nuns complain at me. My mother would teach me new dance moves. It was lot more fun than school would ever be. I felt very special, and who wouldn't want to be home with a gorgeous boy band practicing?

Now in writing this book, I think I realize that I have always wanted to entertain people. When I was very little, I would get up in the middle of the night and do my dance school routines. I was, like, five or six, and was going to dancing school. I had to do a little routine to the song, *When the Red Robin Comes Bob, Bob, Bobbin' Along.* I would get up in the middle of the night and practice. I was worried about my performance. My mom would be sleeping, and she would wake up and say to go back to sleep. But then she'd laugh, and she would tell my Aunt Marian about it. So, I always thought it was funny, because that was me, my personality. I lived in a house with my Uncle Joe who was very funny and a great musician, and I watched him practice his routines. One of his comedy acts was likened to Louie Prima and Keely Smith. All through the pains and struggles of my life there was so much laughter between my friends and me. We just did hysterical things to make people laugh. Thank God I had that sense of humor. It saved me throughout my life.

Bunny Shows Up

I was about eight when my dad showed up at my grade school to pick me up. It was pre-arranged. No one told me he was picking me up with a woman along. He opened the car door, and I got in the back. You might think that the guy who never saw his daughter would let her sit up front with him, but not my father. At first glance at the woman up front, I thought she was a witch, and I was annoyed. Her name was Bunny, and ironically, eventually I ended up adoring her. I guess the reason I thought she was witchy looking was because she didn't look anything like an Italian member of my family. They were all beautiful women, and she was a Russian mixed with some other nationality. They didn't want to say she was Jewish, but she was a Russian Jew. Bunny disarmed me because she said things to me no one else did. That first day, in the car, she turned back to look at me and said, "Look how beautiful she is. Look at her curly black hair, her beautiful face." I can still hear her say these words. She loved me in a way my father could not.

Bunny was a beautiful being and just wonderful. She was so affectionate to me and my siblings. She totally fit in with the family and my brother and his sister. She and my father got married and had my half-brother, Darren. We went out on lots of fun family outings, but I could never, ever mention her name at home or especially to my mother. Well, we were never allowed to mention her or my dad at home, period… in front of my grandfather, God forbid, when he was drinking. It would just create a whole mess and turn into a big scene. And we could never even mention Darren and the fact that we had a half-brother ever. My mom could not handle it or accept it. I was really jealous that my dad and Bunny had an apartment together with Darren, and he's always seemed to dote on Darren and not my brother or sister. My very sick father played us against each other until he died. In fact, right up until the day he died.

Darren was really cute, and Bunny adored him. Even after my father and she broke up, she made sure she got her support money for her son. My mom never got a penny from him. So, Bunny stayed in the family, Sunday dinners, holidays, and all. We just loved her. She was always sweet.

CHAPTER 4

FEAR, GUILT, AND SHAME – JUST PART OF THE GAME

The fear of my grandfather prevented me from ever doing anything bad, or should I say, corrupt, because I loved him more than anything. I also had my own values. I mean, I could have done things for my father that could have earned me something. I never wanted anything from him except love. I had so much PTSD by that point that I never wanted to get arrested or have my grandfather angry at me. What I feared most was losing my grandfather's love. It's a good thing that I wasn't the mafia godmother because I could fantasize about the people I would want to hit and act out the part. But I am my grandfather's daughter, and I cannot really ever kill anyone. There is a saying in the 12-step program, "You're only as sick as your secrets," and that's so true. Many of us would hold secrets in our minds and hearts. It does not serve us. It makes us sick in one way or another. It percolates in our mind, body, and soul. It's a disturbance against life, against our bodies when we hold on to this stuff. Maybe that's what runs in our blood, secrets and guilt. And we were all sick, my dad, my grandmother, the whole damn family. I carried their secrets with me. We all did.

They're not here anymore, weighing me down, but they were weighing me down a lot of my life. I've been carrying the weight of this shame and guilt for a long time. It took a lot to put it down, a lot of therapy, introspection, and spiritual work. And somehow through all the craziness, I was learning about integrity.

Catholics get to go to confession every week to help relieve themselves of the burdens of their supposed sins. But how much can anyone really say in the confessional to the priest? Could anyone safely go and really say anything about what they knew about crimes in the area? What happens if you are a kid and don't really know you are committing a crime? That was a whole situation in and of itself. I had a good friend whose grandfather was a bookie. I did not realize what we were doing or why I had my school uniform on into the evening; it was so uncomfortable being I was overweight. Recently, I found out it was because he told his granddaughter to keep her uniform on, so the cops didn't suspect us! We were running numbers. My grandfather did everything to keep us away from that. I had no clue. We would go to the candy store down the street and the owner would give us a brown bag which had some rolls of paper, some cash and on top of it all, lots of candy. We would pick out what we wanted so I was happy and excited. Who cared what was at the bottom of the bag! All I cared about was the candy.

What I've learned over the years is I have been in shock and experiencing post-traumatic stress syndrome from the beginning. I think it started when he went to jail, when the cops came in, my mom getting hit by my grandfather, all the yelling and constant conflict. I was fucking numb. As an adult, a therapist once told me I was brilliant for what I did, how I took stuff from each aunt and uncle that I liked and left the bad behind.

I am an intuitive and didn't know or understand that for many years. At two, I was able to feel his vibes very strongly and it scared me that my father was a sexual predator. I knew it. And I now know he sexually abused others. He tried to coerce a teenage family member to have a threesome with him and his third wife. My dad was in and out of jail so much, and because my grandfather Lou wouldn't let me see him, I never knew where he was. I wanted to know if he was coming home, because I both loved and missed him, but I also feared him. It was such a confusing feeling for so many years. Even though we prayed for my father, to bring him home, he did not deserve to come back into society, but I didn't understand that yet. I was robbed of a joyous and sweet life because of his actions or inactions to take responsibility for himself and his own life.

I saw him hurt my mom. He wasn't a hitter because he didn't have to hit to get his message across, but he hurt her and me in other ways. I would get so upset and pissed most of the time when he would call from jail. One of us would hang up on the other because I would tell him, as I got older, that he was evil, and he liked being in jail. So, he would say, "You're a fucking bitch," and hang up. I was so sick of, all my life, watching my Grandmother Sue and Bunny and all the women in our lives catering to him. It made me sick to my stomach. In fact, I was sick of all the women who catered to their men, and yet I somehow grew up doing some of the same things, though not in the same ways.

My grandmother Sue, Dad's mother, carried so much pain and guilt about my father, it was as if it was all her fault. She would blame herself. And from the beginning, when I went to therapy, I would come up with all these reasons why I thought my father was the person he was. That was back in the 80s, when they didn't have all the stuff about trauma and what we know now. I would sit there and try to figure him out. I would say maybe it was because his father was an angry man. Maybe it was because my grandfather was a construction worker, and he liked my uncle, Bobby better than my father. My uncle was his best friend because he was also in carpentry, and they were part of the Union. Those two always got along and talked all the time. They both loved Florida. Maybe they didn't understand my father, because he was really artistic and interesting in ways they were not. Maybe it was because when my father was a little boy, my grandmother's own parents were getting old, and it was like she was running two households. She told me that she didn't give him enough attention and it bothered her, and she felt guilty.

I remember all those stories, and she would hold my hand and talk to me. I loved her so very much. I was always so grateful to have any time with her, even if it was going with her to her parents' to help take care of them. I adored her and she adored me. She always called me her number one, which made the others jealous. She always told me this and I loved it and used it to my advantage with my siblings and cousins. It created something in me that I played out over and over in all my personal and work relationships. I always wanted to be number one, and I worked very hard at that. She wanted a daughter, and my grandfather did not want another child. So, when I was born, I filled that need for her. She was angry because my grandfather didn't want another child, so she stopped sleeping with him after I was born. Every night after dinner, we would clean the kitchen. That meant wiping the floor, a job I hated. And she would say to me, "Learn how to drive. Be a leader, not a follower. Be independent, and don't get married."

CHAPTER 5

I LOVE YOU, I HATE YOU

Having a child so young and out of wedlock was very unusual at that time. They used to send girls away who got pregnant. They were always saying things that I overheard that made me feel like I was a mistake, even though my family thought I was a beautiful mistake, and my Grandmother Sue adored me more than anything. And then my parents made a second child, and my grandfather flipped out again. My siblings and I were a burden on them, and no matter how much they loved me and my brother and sister, it was obvious to me, even as a kid, that people should have a better plan. Both my parents were being totally irresponsible. But, of course, the Italians always took care of their own and my grandfather would have never sent his dear little Margie away. I knew he loved her because sometimes he would sing that song, "My Dear Little Margie" to her and she wasn't having it.

We were always surrounded by Italians. They were always helping their families back in Italy. My grandfather who raised me and his brother Joe helped their sisters when they needed it. Italian families are wonderful. They love you to death. They're so great, but when they snap on you and say mean things, it goes on and on like a fucking opera. It's very hurtful. Sometimes it made you question who you were, whether you were loved or not. When they get mad about something, they just lose it. I know now that with my grandfather, losing it was because he was trying to keep me safe, to prevent me from being around my dad and keep me from getting pregnant. I don't think my grandfather really knew the danger of the drugs that were starting to float around. He wanted me to be different than both my mother and father.

It was the messages of guilt and shame that I got from almost everyone around me. The truth is my grandfather loved us living there. He never wanted any of us to leave...ever! On top of that, my grandfather had anxiety about being alone and needed to be surrounded by people all the time. In fact, sometimes, my grandmother had to sit in the bathroom while he showered so he wouldn't feel alone. But of course, my mom's siblings always had something to say about "all my grandparents sacrificed." Some of them were just jealous, and besides that, what would my grandfather do with his money anyway? He'd gamble more or send money to his nephew in Italy to buy more marble floors.

We all have insecurities. My insecurities started showing up in many ways including not thinking I was as good as my peers and cousins. As much as they love you, when people start screaming at you, you don't know where that's coming from. You start losing your dignity. I had to live all these years with that guilt of being my mother's sin and always feeling like the sin itself. I listened to my grandfather say terrible things. Somewhere around five or six years old I started putting on weight. I was very nervous and scared inside and had seen more than any child should have. The stress added to my eating issues. Food is love! Food is safety. Food doesn't scream at you. But food does give you tummy aches and vomiting, and most of all, the loss of control around overeating. And even at such a young age, I started to internalize that. As I got older, I had no clue why I couldn't control my food.

My grandfather screaming at my mother and calling her a whore went deep inside and I'm sure it really hurt her. I often wondered why she always pushed me away. Maybe that's why she never hugged me or touched me in a loving manner. Many years later, I sought help from a therapist known for her expertise in EMDR. I told her that my mother was deeply depressed. I really never felt totally loved or embraced by my mother. I loved that this woman was Italian Catholic and from up north and understood the dynamics of the Catholic Church. If you didn't act pure like the Blessed Mother, you were considered a whore. That "Madonna-Whore complex" is the reason why a lot of men have their girlfriends on the side.

From that therapy, I gained a deeper understanding of my mother and the reasons for her lack of closeness and compassion toward me. Through the information that I was sharing with my therapist, she said that my mom probably couldn't love me the way I wanted her to, because I was her sin, and her father never let her forget it. That behavior probably held her down because she wanted to go everywhere with my father and my grandparents would not let her do that. She would stay in her room a lot of the time when she wasn't working, and she would just sit there. We all tried. My aunts really tried hard to get her out of her shell. But for me, I thought, *What's wrong with me? What's wrong with her?*

I didn't discover the gist of it until I had that EMDR, and the therapist got it out of my system. I have felt unlovable a lot of my life even though I always gave a lot of love! And even when surrounded by love, I couldn't really take it in because I didn't feel lovable. Between being told by my dad that, "Nobody's going to love you if you're fat," my mom never being there for me, and my Uncle Joe punishing me for being fat. I never really felt I was loveable.

I was a lot like my grandfather and didn't want to be like my mother because I wanted him to love me. I saw my grandmother Stella being so docile. I didn't want to be that way. I realized many years later that she was as fierce as a lion. She was a Leo, the lion and fierce in a soft way. I wanted to be more like my grandfather, who had a way with people whether they were coming to the house or the bocce club.

I would emulate men more in business in lots of good ways. I think that attitude is what got me ahead in my career, because I would meet famous people, and I would shake their hand firmly and I would talk to them, refusing to be intimidated. I learned all that from my grandfather, my Aunt Connie, my Uncle Joe, and my father too, in fact.

CHAPTER 6

CRUSHES AND BESTIES

Frankie Brocco played a big part in my childhood. He was very mischievous and very cute. He came from a badass family. His sisters were always there if he got into any trouble, and they wanted to beat the shit out of the nuns. His father owned a hoagie shop on Sixth and Catherine. And he had an uncle named Blue, who was friends with my father.

I don't remember what grade I got him thrown out of school, but I'll get to that. Frankie really liked me, and I liked him, but the kids used to sing a song they called Tessie and Frank. It was sung to the tune of the Elvis Presley song that went, Frankie and Johnny were lovers. The kids would sing Frankie and Tessie were lovers. They called me two-ton Tessie because I was fat. This was very upsetting to me, and I was very, very embarrassed. Not just for me but because I have always been tuned into other people's feelings. I was so embarrassed, but also felt bad that they were making fun of him too, though he didn't seem to care.

We had crushes on each other. He would do crazy stuff though, and it never bothered me. We had the best lemonade stand across from our school, John's Lemonade. In fact, it's still there. One time, he poured cherry lemonade on the top of my head, and it went all over my uniform and my shirt, and I just stood there laughing. My sister Sadie, who was five years younger than I, told me later that she was very scared when he did that until I started laughing. He was very mischievous, but he wasn't mean to me ever. I saw in his eyes a very sweet side to him.

I got him thrown out of grade school by accident. One of his best friends, Cookie, and he would do mischievous things even in class. And I loved that. One day, we're in school and he and Cookie were throwing spit balls at each other. They were hitting me, and I was laughing. I knew he was doing it as a joke. I raised my hand, "Miss Pagano, Miss Pagano," I said. "They're throwing spitballs at me." I didn't know that Father Manzoni, who was from Italy and fucking strict like Hitler was standing in the back door. They both got thrown out of school that day and had to go to St Paul's a few blocks away. Frankie's family lived two blocks from the school, and Saint Paul's was the other direction at least another two blocks. He had to walk all the way to that school every day because they threw him out on my goofing off with them. I was scared shitless because of his sisters. His sisters were badasses, like, really badasses, but they left me alone.

I didn't get to see him all the time anymore, but one day he said that he and Cookie were going to come by my house. By this time, I had gotten chubbier. I wasn't 300 pounds or anything, but I was overweight, and I had this brand-new outfit I was so proud of. I'll never forget it. It was something I had never had before. It was a peach mohair sweater and pants with stir-ups that made me look thinner. I looked so nice, and I was so proud of my appearance that day. I felt like it was a date between us. He came and knocked on my door, but my grandfather was always there. In fact, both my grandmother and grandfather were in the house that day. I said, "I'm going to go out to play with my friends from school. They're coming by." "Who's coming by?" my grandfather asked. And when I said, "Frankie Brocco and Cookie," my grandfather went off the deep end. Everybody knew the Broccos. They were a very tough family. But also, I was never allowed to say boyfriend or that I liked a boy. They all tried to keep me from getting pregnant or having boyfriends. So, I had to go to the door and tell them I couldn't come out. I said, "My grandfather won't let me out." And I was so sad and angry that day. I went to my bedroom screaming and crying. I was banging on the bed. I remember thinking, *when I get older, me and my friend AJ are going to have our own apartment. We're going to have sex and everything with anybody we want.* It was so hard because I really liked Frankie a lot. I loved him as a little girl, and he didn't come around anymore after that. I really didn't see him much after that day. I might have seen him in passing, but he got a girlfriend, and they got married and stayed together. I was happy for him anyway.

I had a lot of friends growing up. Maria was one friend from kindergarten. Her father died and they had to move away. I was sad because he was wonderful to me. He would take us to fancy restaurants because we both had the same birthday, but one day we got caught in my bedroom. We had no clothes on, and we were touching each other. I was feeling things I had never felt before and I was on the verge of something that might have been an orgasm. My grandmother Stella opened the door just at that moment and she started screaming stuff in Italian. She had all these bad words she would use when she was mad. She wasn't a curser, but, oh my god, it was like Mary blessed mother came through, and so we had to put on our clothes, and I got in trouble. The shame I felt that day lasted a long time, and I think may have affected how I dealt with sex for many years. However, it didn't stop me from exploring my sexuality.

I had my girlfriends and guy friends around my neighborhood. I slept a lot at my best friend Josie's house. My grandfather had people he liked and people he did not like me hanging out with. For example, it was okay to be with AJ up to a certain age, but she and I used to sneak off to Atlantic City so eventually she made the "bad for me" list. But my best friends Janet and Rae-Rae were on the good list. I loved them. AJ got caught having sex in the park that was just six doors down from the house, so after that, we really had to sneak around to see one another. People used to hang around in the park after dark drinking and messing around. Word travelled all around the neighborhood every time anything happened. My Aunt Marian knew everything that went on everywhere on the block and surrounding neighborhood, even though she rarely left the house. She had her little salon in the basement full of local people. So, the gossip always got to her, and she would tell my mother and somehow, I would get in trouble. My family absolutely adored Josie. Our families were also friends, especially her grandfather and mine. Her mom, my mom and aunt - on and on.

We loved going to Chinatown which was only about two miles from our house. We would get all dressed up in our Easter outfits with our gloves and our hats and take the bus into Chinatown to one of our favorite restaurants. Sometimes we would go near where my mother worked at Wanamaker's to the Café Teagarden, which was one of the more upscale Chinese restaurants in that area. We knew all the best Chinese restaurants and would eat lunch and then just walk around Chinatown laughing and having fun. We had money from our grandfathers to pay the bill and eat or do whatever we wanted. When it was time to head home, we would get on the 8th Street bus and talk about what the people in the restaurants or on the bus must be thinking about these two little comares. "Comare" is Italian for godmother or close female friend but is also used to describe a mistress (which I didn't know until I watched *The Sopranos*). We thought of a comare as a non-blood relative who was as close as family, someone like your maid of honor. In our neighborhood, comare was also used to poke fun at anyone who dressed or acted like an old lady.

My family always loved and trusted Josie. So, if Josie got cash from her grandfather, it was always easy to sweet talk mine into giving me some spending money if he knew I'd be with Josie. Growing up, I always thought my mom liked Josie more than me. Looking back, I know that it wasn't that she didn't love me, but that I was her sin, and she just was harder on me. But Mom was always very protective of Josie. She could do no wrong in my family.

Josie and My Relationship Growing Up

When we were growing up, my friend Josie's family had a big house, and she had a room like a princess would have with a canopy bed. Her room was on the third floor, but in the next room, her grandfather had a man there taking the street numbers on the phone, who would shove the evidence in a bucket filled with liquid that dissolved the paper if the cops showed up. Her brother and my brother were best friends, but her father took her brother Steve out of the city when we were still in school. Josie stayed at home with her mother.

I would always get Josie in trouble because we would sneak off to places together. As we got into high school years, when we were maybe 14 or 15, they would have bands and concerts that felt like Woodstock at Belmont Plateau. There were mostly hippies there and as much as we wanted to go to them, but we usually didn't have a ride, so I would concoct all these ways to get there. I was always getting her into something that she wasn't allowed to do, and then she'd get in trouble somehow. This happened a lot.

My cousins would be there smoking pot and whatever, and one time I convinced her we were going to take the bus to the park to see the bands. I told her that the cousins would drive us home after the concert. I didn't know that the bus stopped in a really bad neighborhood, basically in the center of the crime area. We got off the bus, and we were scared shitless. But of course, I would never show that I was scared. Josie was cursing me the whole time. "How did you get us into this?" It was just Philly stuff. Finally, we made it to the concert. We had to walk through this bad neighborhood, but we came out alive. Then, on top of it all, we didn't have a ride home. So, we had to hitchhike and get a ride with these weird people. If my family knew what I was doing, they would have put me in a penitentiary or locked me in my bedroom for life.

While in high school, I convinced Josie to go to the concerts at the Spectrum every weekend. I didn't even like Johnny Winters but went to his concert. I did see the Rolling Stones, Rod Stewart many times, and other great bands. On one of these concert excursions, the buses weren't working. They were on strike. I forget how we got there. Maybe somebody dropped us off, but I told her that we had a ride home with Andrew Palumbo and my cousin. Well, Andrew Palumbo had driven his little two-seater car, and we had no way home with him. So, it was late, and we were stuck at the Spectrum. She did not want to call her father or mother, but we tried to call people at a payphone.

I found out much later that Josie was really afraid of her father. She never told me then, but if he would holler at her, she would wet her pants. He was a rage-aholic. She never talked about all of that. Nobody was answering to give us a ride, and we were exhausted. It was really far, but we had to walk all the way home. It was on the other end of South Philly from where we lived. In the 70s, we all wore these big platform shoes. We were all decked out. It used to be fun to walk around the Spectrum and just see who was dressed and what they were wearing, but now we had to get home. We were walking and walking, and then we're sitting and giggling, and then we were crying. She was so scared. I wasn't so much. I just hated that I had to walk like five miles in those shoes. I got punished so much that I was used to being in trouble. We made it home somehow, and it never stopped us from doing more crazy things that we have laughed about it for years.

CHAPTER 7

DON'T BE LATE FOR DINNER

I loved the accolades I would get at restaurants. Many times, the owners or chefs came out and asked if I was a food critic. I could have been a food critic if I wasn't a hairdresser. People have told me to do that for years or to be a comedian.

I still lived on my mother's street even into my 30s, and no matter when I came home, they were up, playing cards. So, even at like 34 years old, after being out all night partying and dancing, I would go to my Aunt Marian's house, and they would have Strombolis; they would have made Zeppole. They would stay up all night, sometimes until four or five in the morning, playing cards, talking shit, drinking espresso, and eating, eating, eating. Even though I had been to a restaurant or a party and had food and drinks, I would come home and try sample a little of everything they were eating because I knew their food was fabulous, comforting, and familiar. I loved being around them. At that point, I had lost all my weight, but still, I was used to this behavior. A lot of times, after dinner, we'd go over to my Aunt Marian's and the adults would start talking and playing cards. And before you know it, Marian would be cleaning up the dishes, and then an hour or so later, she would start making the strombolis. My brother and sister were younger than me and would have some cereal with a little milk before we went to bed, but I would prefer to go over to my Aunt Marian's after dinner. She would always have something I couldn't get at any restaurant, far better than a little cereal. As they got older, they would start doing the same thing I did and would go over to participate in the late-night indulgences.

Dinner was an event in and of itself. When my friends came over, they would be astounded. They said they were never at anybody's house where most nights there were two or three entrees being served. Because my grandfather was a ball breaker and Italian, he had to have a pasta almost every night. In addition, my grandmother might have made chicken or spareribs, meatballs or sausage, or whatever. There were always two or three entrees on the table every night. Sue and my grandfather Tony, my dad's parents, cooked just enough for that night, and maybe some things to take for lunch the next day. But at our house, you never knew who might be dropping by later in the evening; family, guys from the Bocce Club or my Uncle Joe and Grandfather coming home late after they were done working.

As a kid, when I realized that my dad was a sexual perpetrator, I knew he would have sexually abused me, and I also knew that he hated fat people. I believe part of why I got fat was so he wouldn't consider me in that way. It made sense. "Nobody likes a fat girl," he would say. I subconsciously thought, "Good, I'll get fat. You won't touch me, right?"

My grandfather Lou loved to eat too, and he always kept me close. My seat at the dinner table was next to him. There were seven of us and my grandmother would make these big pots of soup and the gravy for the pasta with marrow-filled bones. Yes, we call it gravy, not sauce in my house unless it is a marinara. My grandfather and I would fight over sucking the marrow out of those bones. And he loved it. He would put his arm around me, then he pretended to hit me. Not really hit me, but say, "No, you're taking my bones." That was something between him and me. I knew that made him happy, and I needed his love and protection. So, through this shared love of food, I kept putting on weight. I wasn't exercising as a kid even when I went to school. Members of the family would remark on it. "Oh, she's gaining weight." I did dance and walk a lot to school but that was all the exercise I got.

I became my grandfather's eating buddy at the table. He would bring home cow brains, and my grandmother would roast them. He would give me some to eat, and even though it was gross, I ate them to please him. It was a big deal; not everybody got these. He enjoyed seeing me eat. He didn't want to be the only one eating all the kinds of things alone. I loved sitting right next to him because I loved his big hugs. At the table was my grandfather Lou, with my grandmother and my mother, my Uncle Joe, my sister, Sadie, who was a tiny, little thing, and my brother Louis. My siblings didn't eat a lot and how they would get rid of the food was to feed it under the table to the dogs. But not me. I made sure every morsel got into my mouth. And both our dogs ultimately died of obesity.

Wherever I was in the neighborhood, I still had to be at the dinner table at either house by 5 p.m. And of course, I was always expected at the big Sunday Italian breakfast, lunch, and dinners. It was always church followed by family coming over to visit. At the Mallace family house, my grandmother Stella would get up at 6 or 7 in the morning. She would begin making her meatballs and start her sauce with pork, sausage, beef, and braciole, and she would let it all sit on the stove simmering for hours. She would walk to her 7:00 mass and come home to resume making the meatballs and the gravy. We all went to church at different times. After church, when everybody was back, my grandmother made this big frittatona con carne with eggs, cheese, and pieces of the different meats. We all sat around and feasted. Later that evening, by around 5 p.m., we would have dinner.

At the Agnes family, my grandfather would get up and make the gravy and his was different because it was more of a Sicilian gravy with a stick of pepperoni in to make it spicy. He would like to take us for rides afterwards and show us the buildings for projects he worked on. I loved that, and I've always had a profound interest in architecture. And then we would go visit one of his siblings. Also, Bunny, my dad's second wife who I adored, my half-brother Darren, Uncle Bobby and his wife, my Aunt Rita and my cousins, and sometimes my two siblings came over.

Crime and Punishment

As I got older, my uncle Joe who I loved, was unfairly handed the task of being a father figure. He was one of the key figures in my life, and he would punish me for gaining weight. Later he started punishing me for other things. I got used to that punishment, and I actually looked forward to it because somehow it felt like he loved me and cared. In a lot of ways, I could trust his punishments not to be violent. When my mom would punish me, she'd hit me or pull my hair. She would hit me so hard that my lip or nose would bleed. She was very rough with me. I hated being home alone with just her when my grandmother Stella needed to be away.

My Uncle Joe would punish me for answering back or things like that, which made more sense to me. He was in a boy band, and he traveled so he went away one summer. I think I was about six, and I did something bad. I don't remember what I did. I probably answered somebody back and or maybe hit my brother. Who knows? And he said, "You're punished." He was doling out my punishment from fucking Los Angeles. And I was okay with that. My God, who wants to be punished at six? My mother was 16 when she came home with me. Though her brother was only fourteen, he became like a father figure, since my dad wasn't in the picture. I knew he had protective feelings for me. And what he knew of being a father was that fathers punish their kids. "No, you can't do this. No, you can't do that." He just got in the habit of it. Maybe it was a way for him to keep me from getting pregnant. He likely saw that they were all afraid that I would be bad and get pregnant, like my mom. It's understandable. Punishing me was a form of keeping me in a chastity belt of sorts. After all, my mom knocked out three kids in a row with a guy they couldn't stand.

No matter how fucking angry I would be, no matter how much I cried when they punished me, even later in life, no matter how many people in business tried to stop me, or people who acted like they were better than me, I always saw myself as special. Despite my insecurities, I think that attitude, that belief in myself and the encouragement of my grandmother Sue who always told me I was special and important, was the only counterbalance I had against the damage done to me as a kid. Even as a little kid, I always thought about ways to make money or do business in everything I did. I wanted to be successful, and I was determined to make it happen. So, as I was getting fatter by the minute, and I believed it kept my father away from me, from abusing me. It has been a very long road with my eating disorder of which I will talk about in my next book.

From MAFIA PRINCESS *to* LESBIAN CHIC

CHAPTER 8

BIG DRUG BUST

In 1968, during my high school years, I was going back and forth a lot more between both sets of my grandparents' houses. They lived eight blocks apart and now I could go see my grandparents Sue and Tony any time I wanted to. My grandfather Lou couldn't control me or stop me from seeing my other grandparents anymore. And lots of time was spent at my aunt Teresa's, my grandfather's sister's house which was right in the middle of both grandparents' homes. I went to my aunt Teresa's almost every day to hang out with my cousins and their friends. My aunt's house was right behind the most famous bakery in all of Philadelphia and still is, Termini Brothers Italian Pastries. They had unbelievable world class pastries just like Ferrara's in New York and sometimes on holidays would have live opera or Italian music while people shopped. Mr. Termini sometimes would send over freshly made donuts to my aunt's early in the morning.

There were lots of drugs floating around the city in those days. I really wasn't crazy about pot, but I smoked it just to be sociable with my cousins and friends. Everybody would be sitting shoulder to shoulder because the basement at the house was small. Music was always playing, some of the guys would be playing their bongo drums, and we all shared whatever we had. Little did I know who was at the helm of all these drugs. My dad, Louis Agnes Sr., was around more during this period than others. Somehow, he had managed to stay out of jail a while.

I was trying to figure things out: school, boys and girls, life, my friends, lots of new friends from high school. Do I go to Wildwood and with my cousins and his friends? Or do I go to my favorite place, Atlantic City (which was way before the casinos came in)? We all went to concerts at The Spectrum almost every weekend. We saw Mick Jagger, Sly and The Family Stone, James Taylor, and Rod Stewart. Rod Stewart was my all-time favorite back then.

One Sunday, I was informed that my father had a new girlfriend that he brought back from Los Angeles, and he was bringing her over to Sunday dinner. She was a flight attendant. I was a junior in high school, and very unhappy with my weight and my curly hair. I certainly didn't feel very pretty. So, when my dad brought Margie over, this very pretty, petite blonde, demure looking to be about 21, not much older than I was, I just wanted to spit in his face. When I was twisted, I could be a real bitch. Paul would say my mouth was as bad as my father's silencers. Well, I was furious. She was also very shy and timid. She was everything I was not. I wondered if she knew what she was in for. Bunny, who was then divorced from my dad, was there that day, but she didn't care because she knew how to deal with my dad. She was tough and street smart, but she had made a better woman out of herself. She didn't let him get away with anything, especially when it came to her getting her money. Everybody loved Bunny. My dad paid child support for Darren, but not for my siblings and me. Margie did everything she could to befriend me and make me happy, but I was not having it. Anyway, everybody really liked Margie, but I just wanted to stick the fork in her. Unfortunately, she didn't have an ounce of body fat to stick it in to. The poor thing, she was beautiful, sweet, and once he was locked up, she would drive all the way to go visit him in jail.

Margie became a part of our lives, and she was good to me, unlike my asshole dad. He was so mean, and he forbade Margie to teach me how to drive his new Caddy. Meanwhile he had a Corvette and a Jaguar as well. So, you know what? Bunny and my cousin Linda taught me. Then one day, I was told that Margie was going to take me, my grandmother, and one of my best friends to the shore. I was excited because there was a cute guy there that I liked. At the last minute, my father had her take us to New Hope, an artisan village in northeast Pennsylvania instead, and I was pissed. He made reservations at the Bucks County Playhouse for us, and I was really angry, so much so that I made my grandmother cry in the restaurant. I asked if I could sit in the car while they were eating lunch. My grandmother was so, so sad. I had a crochet project I was working on, and my scissors "slipped" and just "happened" to cut the seat belts in the back of the brand-new Caddy. I don't even know if he ever saw this, but I never heard a word. Maybe he thought my brother Darren did it. Or maybe they never saw it because who sits in the back? And back then we really didn't use seat belts. I just wanted to be in Atlantic City on the Million Dollar Pier and the beach, but I was stuck doing what he wanted instead as always.

It might have been the first time I went to New Hope. I really did miss out. By that point, Margie had moved into the stunning white house my father lived in with only one bedroom. Obviously, he didn't want anyone to stay over unless they were having a three-some.

When I watched how my dad cared for Bunny and now Margie, it would really hurt me because I couldn't remember a time with him where he treated my mom and my siblings with such attention. Yes, he took us to very nice places, but he doted on Darren. I felt sad and guilty that my mom was home alone with the family and never had a boyfriend, and here I was having a good time at my grandparents and going out on the town. I had a job through high school at Silverman's Bridal Shop on 6th and South St. There were two Italian ladies that worked there that I knew and one of them, our neighbor, got me the job. I really loved the job. It was fun. I loved dressing the window mannequins, and I learned a lot helping the salesgirls pick out dresses and style the brides. And I also learned the art of salesmanship. I've always been a great salesperson and somehow, I chalked it up to working and helping the sales ladies there. They were ruthless.

In the 1950s through the 1970s, most of the bridal shops and stores that were there were owned by Jewish people and the Italians had the hoagie shops. Along South Street, there were very famous delis, and all the Jewish ladies I worked with loved that. During this time, I learned a lot about Jewish culture and food. Later, the area began to change into a more artisan and hippie hang out. Some great fine dining places began to pop up as well as cool bars, music venues, hip salons, and fabulous clothing stores.

Well, somewhere toward the end of my junior year, my grandfather, Tony, was supposed to pick me up from work and when I called to say I was finished, I was told that my grandmother's friend Rita was going to pick me up instead. Rita picked me up and told me that someone got arrested in the neighborhood and there were cops and FBI agents hanging around. When she dropped me off at the front door of my house, I saw lights blinking down the street and cop cars and FBI agents all along 9th St. When I walked into the house, my grandparents looked distraught and a mess. I looked at my grandparents and thought "What the fuck?" It always broke my heart to see them like that. They had been putting up with my father's troublemaking and crimes since he was a teenager. My grandmother said, "Your father got picked up because he shipped a bunch of hair dye from Italy." I didn't know what to say or do. Was she saying this because that's what they told her, or she didn't want to tell me it was a drug bust? But I looked at her like, *really? Give me a break.* I wanted to walk over to my father's house. She stopped me and told me my father wasn't there and they had already taken him and a few others in, including Margie. You know, I could never figure out my dad for years. I didn't even know about psychopaths, sociopaths, and narcissists back then. I just thought he was fucking stupid, but he really wasn't. I learned over the years that he was brilliant in many ways. He didn't drink or use meth even though he manufactured it, but I know he smoked pot. I think his drug of choice may have been cocaine. He had no impulse control and thought of many crazy—but sometimes brilliant—things. Was that the coke at work or just the way he was wired?

In this particular bust, doctors, cops, and political people were involved. My father had flown a big statue of a famous doctor in from Amsterdam, and it was registered to go to Dr. Silverstein. To clarify, there were two Dr. Silversteins. They were brothers, but one was straight up and law abiding and the other was not. My Dr. Silverstein gave diet pills to me when I was 13 years old. It came to light that the statue was full of hashish. Someone totally ratted my dad out. The detectives followed the truck with the statue to the house that evening from the airport. Dad and Uncle Bobby had designed the house together. Dad had the first meth lab in the neighborhood in that garage. No one told me that until after my dad died. Back then I would get in his face about stuff, especially when he was in prison, but by the time he got out he would have forgotten all about it. Sometimes I think he liked when I got cocky with him. It's crazy, but I always felt like I was his favorite. He knew I was strong in a lot of ways, and he couldn't play me. The house was an ultra-modern design, all white and different than any other house in South Philly. The front door was next to the garage, and there were a lot of steps going up to the second level. I think he must have planned it that way so if the cops busted in, they would have a lot of steps to run up. The second floor opened up to a beautiful family room with sliding glass doors and a patio and steps that led outside. The windows in the dining room were very slim and long. We could see out, but no one could really see in. Everything was modern and plush with white leather couches, fabulous art, and lots of glass. And in between those two rooms was this beautiful, winding staircase that led to the luxurious shower and then only one big, huge bedroom.

My dad had one art piece I will never forget which was on the wall leading up the staircase. It was a huge, hand-painted picture of God and the devil playing chess with human beings for pawns. It was painted on two pieces of glass put together with silver screws a bit off centered. I always pictured it as a great scene for a movie with the cops racing up those steps with their hatchets, the painting in view, and the Stones' "Jumping Jack Flash" playing in the background.

Dad had a fake wall behind the bed and that's where he stashed all his paperwork with people's names and their records of what he sold. There was lots of money; some real, some counterfeit. When he realized he was going to be caught and the cops were on their way, Dad started flushing the records of people and whatever else he needed to get rid of down the toilet. By the time the cops got up there, the toilet couldn't flush any more. The cops tried to get at it, and they chopped up the toilet in this gorgeous bathroom. Whoever ratted him out, ratted him out good, because the cops knew where certain things were hidden behind the wall. There were also other people there with him, including Marty Hess, who turned on him and went under the witness protection program, and another couple that turned went away and I never saw them again. They took Margie and others who were driving the van to jail as well.

After the big drug bust, there was a whole week of posting bail, but I just went about my business. I couldn't deal with all his theatrics. He had my grandmother doing all kinds of things like writing to judges about his "good character." One time, I walked into the kitchen and saw Jim Tayoun talking with my grandfather about what he could do to help my dad. Jim was a crooked politician in the Pennsylvania House of Representatives. I remember my grandmother lighting candles for my dad, saying masses.

The next few days and weeks were full of news coverage on Channel 6, Channel 10, and Channel 3. It apparently was the biggest drug bust they ever had in Philadelphia back then. I was so numb from all the other things that happened to me that I was just kind of floating through life. Conveniently, Dad married Margie, obviously to keep her from testifying against him.

So, the drug bust happened in my junior year. My dad was able to stay out of prison that whole year. He must have posted bail and just stayed out until the trial finally happened. Trials can take forever, and especially in cities like Philadelphia, a trial could take a lifetime. Meanwhile, it was my senior year in high school, but it was just all about him and it really still sometimes makes me angry if I think about it. One of my friends wanted to take my father to the senior prom and my father laughingly suggested that he would go with us and Lee would be my date. NO WAY! But he did rent us a limo to take my friends and I to the prom.

He gave me a fabulous party for my high school graduation at his house. One of the highlights was this big, beautiful, silver fountain overflowing with chocolate, like you see at hotels. He invited a few of his friends and a few people there were sketchy. Then, during the summer after my graduation, on August 7th, Marty Hess was murdered.

From MAFIA PRINCESS *to* LESBIAN CHIC

PART 2

Escaping my Italian Prison

From MAFIA PRINCESS *to* LESBIAN CHIC

CHAPTER 9

TRIALS AND TRIBULATIONS

S eptember 27, 1972, was a lot more to deal with than usual. The Philly summer heat was cooling down, but my temperament was not. My dad was out on bail from the drug bust and then was implicated in the murder of Marty Hess. There were two big trials planned back-to-back. Once again, my ability to enjoy the beautiful Philly fall with all its wonderful festivals and events was marred by all the different lawyers and judges and trial preparation.

Living at 907 Sigel St. and the Agnes household was usually my safe and quiet place when it was just my grandparents, my siblings, and me. Let's just say as long as my father wasn't around, it was great. I was dealing with the usual post high school angst. I had wanted to go to cosmetology school for many years. I worried that my mom didn't have that kind of money and "poor Louis Agnes, Sr." with three new cars in his garage wouldn't pay a dime. In hindsight, it was never about what he could do to help us, it was always what we could do for him. He always had a scheme and everything he did for us was to establish an alibi for one of his many crimes. He did that with my graduation party and the limousines that he gave us for prom.

I hated going up before the judge or jury. And even though he was married to Margie, Bunny was still his greatest cheerleader.

During the trial, Bunny attended, and when there was a break, we would go to the ladies' room. Bunny would make sure there was no one in the room with us, and she would give the inside info on the jurors or whatever shady stuff was going on behind the scenes. I'm surprised those bathrooms weren't wired, but I guess it was the 1970s. The trials for the drug bust happened and my dad was convicted and given time along with all the other guys involved. He also had more time tacked onto his sentence because he had counterfeit money on him during his arrest.

I had started Martin Anthony Academy Cosmetology School and moved over to the Wilfred Academy and was also dating Paul that fall. That brought me lots of fun and joy. Some of the guys in class were Italian gay boys from South Philly. One of my dearest friends was Joe Spadarro and the other was Chip De May. They were two of the most gorgeous guys in the class. Joe was very funny, and he called me Picasso because of the way I did my make-up. Chip went on to travel the world doing photo shoots of famous people, models, and stars.

Lots of nights, we would all be in the gay boy clubs dancing away. Of course, I was having the time of my life. I had been going to the gay clubs in Atlantic City from when I was 15 or 16 and then there were the drag clubs on 13th St. and Locust. Most of the clubs were owned or at least financed by people like my dad and his friends. I would sometimes see some of the guys that hung with dad pop in and out of the gay clubs. There was one big club called Harlow's named for a beautiful trans woman who was the hostess there. She was from South Philly, born Richard Finocchio, a very effeminate boy who really looked as close to a girl as could be. She won all kind of pageants and in 1972, she was one of the first people to surgically transition. I don't remember hearing anything bad about Harlow from my father or anyone at the house, and I was used to Francine from the neighborhood. Also, I had several friends at Wilfred Academy that were starting to transition, and I became very supportive of them.

Club Harlow was a fabulous place, and sometimes when I would go, there were a lot more straight people than I expected. My father being one of those. Straight and gay people came together, and it was kind of like Studio 54, with a mixture of every kind of person in the city. The booze and drugs were always flowing. It was the first club of its kind in Center City Philly, very classy and all the coolest people would go there. My dad would go there sometimes, but I never ran into him. I preferred the music at the other gay clubs. Camac's Bathhouse was right there where a lot of construction guys went for steam baths, saunas, and massages. A few times, my dad brought me and Margie so we could get treatments. I had a kickass party in there in my 30s. Meanwhile, although I felt like I was on the verge of a nervous breakdown from my father, there were also fun times that I admit I had with him. It's sad. He really taught me a lot of things. I learned that tipping people and getting to know them helped to get a better table. He taught me how to properly treat waitstaff including a maître d in a club, restaurant or casino to get that next level of service. I learned how to navigate a lot of adult experiences I would never have learned to do without him; never learned "the ropes." He had so many opportunities to have a great life, be a great husband and father, but he always blew it for all of us, and more importantly, for himself.

My dad did eventually go to jail for the drugs, but he didn't go to jail for the murder of Marty Hess. So, he had kind of concurring trials, almost like one trial right after the other. He was implicated in the Marty Hess thing, but nothing could be proved. The cops that were involved were charged with the murder.

He was married to Margie by the time he finally went to prison, and I would sometimes go visit him with her. I remember this one time there was a glass partition between us, and she apparently didn't do something he wanted her to do regarding the Muslim prisoners he was in with. My dad started some kind of shit with the Muslims. He was banging on the glass, and he was so angry, like he wanted to kill her. I knew he wanted her to bring money to some people to stop the fight in jail. Somehow, he created a fucking riot in the prison. I remember saying, "I'll go with you" putting me on the line. We went to some house in a very scary neighborhood and did what he asked.

Sometimes he went to solitary. He was always starting shit, and I'm sure the guards took good care of him because of all the lasagnas and meatballs they got from my grandmother. You know, that's why I think he was so well taken care of in prison. Sometimes I really do think it was safer for him to be in there than on the streets because people were getting killed. I'm not sure he was really worried because he had another whole life in there, honest to God, but nobody ever hurt that man.

It wasn't until that fateful summer when Marty Hess got killed, that Paul and I really reconnected. During that week, while my grandparents weren't around, I hosted parties. The neighbors were buzzing about the big presence of lesbians at the parties. The week after when my grandparents had returned, Paul had heard about the parties, and he came by late at night and we sat on the steps and talked until 1-2 in the morning. Over the next few weeks, he stopped by more frequently. We eventually started dating again. He was fun to date because he loved going to shows and nice restaurants, and most of the time, he kept me laughing. As things progressed, we talked about getting married and having kids.

Paul became a big part of my life. I knew him from very young and Paul was always very generous. For example, we were both big Diana Ross fans and he bought us tickets to see her at the Latin Casino in 1969. He was 15. I was 14, and I think either his brother or father was going to drive us from Philly to Jersey. Except that was the time her poodles died in her dressing room, and she cancelled the rest of her tour.

I remembered that when Paul was a child, he was funny, generous, and I always knew he liked me, even as a young boy. I put away the fact that in between there, he became a little violent and would chase after me. I had heard rumors of things he'd done, but I put all that aside because part of my memories of him were warm and fuzzy. None of us are just one dimensional. He could be very nice and loving most of the time. Things would be going great, but then I never knew when something would irritate him, and his temper would flare. One time, while Paul and I weren't talking, I was walking to Sunday mass alone and he was behind me. He tried to talk to me, but I ignored him, so he threatened to hit me. He didn't touch me, but I knew if I told anyone that he threatened to hit me he could have gotten seriously hurt. By that time, they had moved around the corner on Mifflin St. and our paths didn't cross a lot anymore. I was hanging with my besties and my cousins and their friends all through high school. And then I had my curiosity with lesbians and bisexual girls.

It was so hard and unpredictable, and I really didn't realize he was an alcoholic for quite a while after we were dating. When bad things happened, I think I was kind of in shock that he hit me, and then there would be all the apologizing and all the sex and everything else. I'd think, "That isn't who he really is." I had to come to a place where I finally said, "This is who he is, at least more of the time than not, and I won't accept that behavior anymore." It's not easy to get there, but with a lot of therapy and hard work, I knew I wanted and deserved better. I had to craft a way to get there. I wanted my dignity back. It was destroyed by some of my family years before. One of the most important traits I had was resilience and I knew what I wanted. Though I will always be a work in progress, I am always striving and learning to get to know myself and others better.

Cosmetology school started in the fall of '72. Martin Anthony Academy was the best hair academy in the city at the time. There were gorgeous men and women and a few of us had crushes on each other. One of the guys, Michael, liked me a lot and was vying for my attention. Paul caught on, and of course, he was jealous and pissed. At that point, I knew he had a propensity for violence, but I was having so much fun with him that I was in denial. I wasn't really on to his use of alcohol, but I knew he was using diet pills. Sure enough, it all reared its ugly head, and I don't really remember the first time he hit me. You'd think I would? The first time he hit me, my self-worth, which was already pretty low, plummeted. From the first time he hit me, I knew I wasn't marrying him and definitely wasn't having children with him.

I already had been used to physical and verbal abuse from my grandfather. I knew that when Grandpop came home drunk, and if he was twisted, he would holler at one of us and go off. It was either me, my mother, or my grandmother. Sometimes he would punish me, and I would run upstairs and cry. He didn't do this when my Uncle Joe was around because my uncle would stop him from fighting with my grandmother and being abusive. He was always furious with my mom, and he'd hit her. But my grandfather would call me down and apologize and put his arms around me. He would try to make it up to me by ordering our favorite takeout from the Chinese Palace. He would let me get my favorite things. We always bonded around food. All the while I was choking down the sobs, the fear, and the anger. Paul did the same things after a fight. He would bring me presents, sweet talk me into make-up sex, and order our favorite takeout food. I think part of the reason I stayed with Paul was my bestie Debbie moved away to Colorado. And my other bestie was getting married and planning their wedding and all the things I used to do with them weren't the same. And that the pattern was so familiar. I knew there were a lot of places I wanted to see and things I wanted to do. My besties had their own things going on. I had always had fun with Paul in the past, and he liked travelling and doing fun things. So, he seemed like a good prospect to explore life with.

Little did my father know what was going on at that point. I was well aware of Paul's violent tendencies from very young. One summer, the men were all outside on Sigel Street sitting around a table playing cards and drinking beer. I was at my grandmother's house and all of a sudden, I heard shouts and screaming from these men. So, I ran out right away and there was Paul fighting with these men. He was trying to beat one of our neighbors up. I heard one of the guys call him a "Spic" – a derogatory word for Spanish people. All the men couldn't hold him down. He was wild. It was crazy, and it really frightened me when I saw that. Somehow the guys broke up the fight, and Paul went inside his house. But from that point on, that picture always stayed with me, and I was really scared of him. Not only was I scared of him, but I was also scared for how crazy he could be if he ever got in a fight with someone in my family.

I still had lots of friends and a lot of them loved Paul. My family loved Paul, and he was generous to my mom and family. There were all different trials going on with my dad. My brother was using drugs and drinking. Life was really hard for me and the worst part was hiding Paul's abuse. I really couldn't talk to anyone about it. I couldn't talk to anyone about my dad, and I just kept gaining weight. I didn't understand what was wrong with my mom. I learned from early on that it wasn't safe to reveal anything about my family or my life. I felt like shit, but all the time was pretending that I was okay and was busy making everyone laugh.

Paul and I went to the Atlantic City shore and other places. We took some nice vacations to Puerto Rico, Canada, California, and other spots. I remember one time we were in Annapolis, Maryland, for the Fourth of July on the water. It was so beautiful, yet I remembered feeling so lonely inside. I started to be aware of these empty feelings inside. As it kept happening, I sat up and took notice.

Debbie's mom and boyfriend had a beautiful place in Ventor, New Jersey, and they were always wanting us to come. And I really missed Debbie because she and I would always stay at their shore house since high school. And then a few strange things started to happen. On Memorial Day, we were supposed to head down to the shore in the morning, and Paul was nowhere to be found until we got a call from him in the hospital. Apparently, when he was driving home that night, he was stopped at a light, and two guys asked him if he had a match for their cigarettes. Then they jumped into his car and drove him around and beat him up and dumped him at the airport. The cops found him and brought him to the hospital. Of course, his father and brother picked me up and took me to the hospital with them and they were furious. They left to find the car and the two guys before the cops did. Luckily the cops found the guys and they were from 2nd St., which at the time was where all the "Medigans" lived. That's the Italian term for Irish, Polish, and any white, non-Italian Americans. Back then, they weren't really allowed in the Italian neighborhoods, and we didn't go over to their side. There were many fights and killings because of that. Back then, the neighborhoods were segregated, Polish in one area, Irish, Lithuanians, and then there was a crossover with the Jewish people and African Americans. There was a trial for these guys, and they got some time. But somehow, I did not believe Paul's story.

At that time, we had he had a Chevy Camaro. It was a very pretty car, but there was always something happening to it. I tried not to hit the potholes, but it was more than that. One time I came out to find the car banged up, not from a car accident, but like somebody kicked it. Of course, he tried to blame me. I chalked it up to someone or kids who were just jealous because it was such a cool car. And then there were intermittent beatings. And then there was one time when Paul really hit me and even though I tried to hide the bruises, Bunny, my stepmother, saw them and she was pissed off and said very strongly, "You know, if your dad ever sees those marks, he will kill him." Of course I knew that. That's one of the reasons I never let anyone know. My godfather, Uncle Bobby, and Paul had some bad blood between them, so I knew not to tell him, or it would get back to my father. One of the times Paul hit me, and I was just done with him, so he put himself in a rehab. It was a beautiful rehab, and I did go see him. Sure enough, he got himself thrown out. Somehow, he and a few other guys snuck out and crossed over Roosevelt Boulevard and went drinking. He got thrown out and showed up at my door and had bandages all over his left arm. His psychiatrist called and told me that Paul was cutting his arms with a plastic knife, and that he wasn't really trying to commit suicide. My heart sunk to the ground, and I just was like, *I gotta deal with this again.* I was so emotionally manipulated by him and really had this fear in my head that my father would kill him and then his dad would retaliate and hurt someone in my family. What I didn't know at the time was how powerful my dad was, and that people really feared him.

Paul was such a big part of my life and because we didn't have kids, we were always taking out his nieces and nephews who I still adore. We had so much fun with the kids, taking them all over to different events in Philly and Jersey, and to the Country Club for swimming and I really liked having this whole family thing. The beatings did not happen on a regular basis, so when he would plead and say he'd never do it again, somehow, I believed him. I'm not making excuses or minimizing what he did, but I used to tell myself, well, it was only a slap. But then one time he threw a brick at my back. I broke up with him and it lasted a year. In that year, I had the time of my life. I taught arts and crafts on an Italian cruise ship with gorgeous Italian men and flirted my way through. I had so much fun. I had just lost 90 lbs. and felt really good about myself. When I came back, I returned to chaos. I chose to fall back into his trap of "I'll never hit you again, I'm so sorry." And so, I went back shortly after.

Fireworks on the Fourth of July

Paul's birthday was during the 4th of July weekend, and he wanted me to stay home with his drunk ass. I wasn't about to give up another one of my 4th of July weekends because of something he was doing, so I went to the swim club with Bunny without him and he was furious. There were no cell phones back then, so we had no way of calling each other. I went to Bunny's after swimming and called Paul to pick me up, which was a very wrong move. I heard in his voice the minute I got into the car how drunk he was. I took a lot of crazy chances with my life and that night was a big one.

As soon as I got into the car, he was seething and drunk. He stopped on 10th and Morris and wanted me to go into the store to buy him cigarettes. We were only four blocks from home. I thought about going into the bar and asking for help, but the bar was packed for the 4th of July weekend. I didn't want to go in and draw attention because I was afraid that he would come in after me and cause a scene. I didn't even know who to call at that point because I was so scared. I got back in the car and just prayed.

When we got to his house, he didn't park in front. Instead, he pulled up on the corner of 9th and Mifflin by Southwark School, where no one could hear anything. Then, he started punching me and trying to bash my head into the windshield. He was so furious with me for not spending the day with him. He was grabbing me by the strap of my denim dress and thank God the shoulder strap ripped, and I was able to get free from him and out of the car and run into a neighbor's house.

I was so scared I was shaking and embarrassed. They were very nice to me and gave me ice packs for my face and head. I didn't know who to call. My dad's house was literally a half a block away. I didn't want to call him though, so I called my cousin Sammy. He is the one I said that I went to nursey school with, who made me feel safe even at the age of four. I could have called one of his brothers. We all were very close, but I think he was the toughest of them all and I knew he could handle himself. Sammy came in and I was shaking, and he wanted me to go out with him to his car. He was taking me back to his house with his wife Sara and two kids. I was really, really scared to walk out to the car and my cousin Sammy assured me that nothing would happen.

I never thought what may have gone on in the back scene because Sammy kept telling me he had it covered when we were getting in the car. His wife always joked that maybe he took his shotgun or was carrying something else. But the other thing was that Sammy's dad had a good friend who lived right across from Paul and around the corner from where we were. Sammy may have called him; I just didn't know. But I know I got in the car. After that, Paul never touched me again or threatened me or anything. Right after that, I started therapy, and he called to tell me he started therapy as well and would never ever hit me again and he never did. I didn't think anything of the fact that he stopped automatically and never hit me again.

I did go back, yes. I was very sick those years and addicted to him and his drama just as much as anyone who's addicted to pot, drugs, alcohol, or sex. So, life moved forward, and Paul never hit me, and I thought he was getting better with therapy. We both had our own places, and it was easy for him to hide his alcoholism and his addiction to porn and to those phone sex numbers. I found his phone bill and saw the numbers and how much they were. I confronted him and of course he tried to blame me because I did not want to have sex with him. All the damage to the relationship was done, and I just wasn't feeling it. I had started therapy, and my self-worth improved, so I refused to let him blame me for any of that. I told my therapist how he never hit me anymore or got crazy and she said that men who are abusers like that just don't wake up and stop hitting women. That it was very rare. That's why women or even men go to shelters or move out of the state for a while. I didn't put two and two together for a long time. I just really thought that his therapy was going well.

We got a new car from my dad's friend who owned a car dealership. It was a very nice car and once again the car was getting banged up. I don't know why it always seemed to happen when I used it, except this one night I had been out with a friend. I called to ask Paul to pick me up and he sounded shaky, and he said he that something was wrong with the car, so she dropped me off at his mother's because he was still living at home.

At this point, I went in, and he was hysterical, crying. He told me the car was totally smashed, the windows, everything. He was shaken and scared. Then, he finally told me what was going on. He confessed to me that he was calling this straight guy named Tony who I knew and had a crush on when I was in high school. The guy was totally straight and married, and I think he had kids at that point. Paul would get drunk, call the guy's landline, and then go to his actual house. He lived a few blocks away and Paul would call Tony from the street and proposition him. I was in shock. But then certain things all started to make sense to me about the car and other things. I was mortified and totally upset. I felt the worst feeling I had ever felt and all the while my dad kept asking me, "What's going on with that car? Why is it always smashed?" And I didn't know. My father probably knew something was going on. And even though I knew at this point, I would never rat out the guys who were doing it. Tony was besties with my cousins, and we had all hung out together all through high school. And besides, it was all Paul's fault.

So, here I was in the middle of all that shit. I was already growing and changing. I was working in a salon close to Wharton Business School. And these people that lived in the nearby loft apartments were fabulous. I started cutting a bunch of those guys' hair and one in particular was a gorgeous, tall Italian guy, Lenny, from New York. I realized how much I was missing out on when Lenny came in to get his haircut. I could feel his eyes just searing through me. I was so miserable and torn up inside. I was still overweight and very insecure with myself. There were a bunch of guys that came to me to get their hair cut who were just gorgeous, super smart, and had some money. They were flying all over the place and one of them was getting married in Switzerland, and they were all going. I was really envious and here I was in this very dead-end relationship. All through this heartache and pain, I was growing leaps and bounds. I couldn't go any faster with all the problems swirling around me, my dad, my depressed mom, my siblings, and Paul. Even at my highest weight, I would still go to work all dressed up and wear stiletto heels on some days. I was always light on my feet and a great dancer, "all in high heels," as they say.

Well, I had talked to my cousin to get Tony's number. I had to talk to them about Paul and the car and my dad. Tony told me they were going to beat up Paul pretty badly. They had bats and chains. Somehow Paul got away and ran into his mother's house, and they didn't want to go in there after him. I thanked Tony and told him I appreciated him leaving Paul alone.

I changed the number of days I would spend with Paul and threw myself into evening classes and photography, darkroom art classes at Fleischer's Art School in Philly. I needed to wean myself away from him.

And then one night after I dropped Paul off at his house, I took the car home. Well sure enough, I got a call about 12:00 a.m. from him, and he said that he barely could dial my phone number. He was hysterical. Some one shot him in the right shoulder while he was walking through the door. My intuition was so strong that for a year I dreamt that something was going to happen to him, and he wouldn't be able to contact me. When Paul got shot, I realized that's what the dream was about. He went to the hospital in an ambulance, his brother and father took me to the hospital, and they had him in surgery. They said he might lose use of his right arm. The right arm seemed to signal to me that it was because he used to hit me or because of the phone calls he used to make to Tony.

More Paul stuff

So, many of the years I felt really bad for Paul. His parents were very abusive to him. His mother was unstable "cray-cray" and yet sometimes loveable. She grew up in Texas and had a hard life. She was sexually abused by her father. Paul's father cheated on her, and he was a real bastard. He was a very, very hateful human being, and he never provided them with enough money. Paul couldn't even go to college because there wasn't enough money and had to go to work right away. They often didn't have heat or electricity in the house.

We both attended Catholic high schools. Bishop Neuman was for the boys, and St. Maria Gorettis, mine, for all girls. Paul had a very hard time getting the tuition money from his dad and so he got jobs after school. In his senior year, he barely scraped up the money so he could graduate. He got a great job at Bell Telephone company in Philadelphia after high school. Paul was half Spanish and half Sicilian, so that could account for some of his temper. I'm not saying that all Spanish and Sicilians are like that, but the combination could be lethal. He got teased a lot about being Spanish and called bad names like spic, which is a derogatory name for any Spanish person. Paul also claimed that he was sexually abused by his mother and that really put a toll on his life and his anger. My heart really hurt for him many times over. Over the years, I learned that those feelings of wanting to take care of him and makeup for his hurt was more about "codependency," a very overused word. When I finally read the book *Codependent No More*, it started to change my life.

And then I went to Al-Anon. That was the program that really changed my life. I have always said that Al-Anon saved me. And that my guru Ma made my life worth living. What I learned in Al-Anon were the three Cs. I didn't Cause his disease. I certainly could not Control it, and I couldn't Cure it. I grew up learning to think I could fix everyone, or at least try. I was trying to heal Paul, but it was me who needed to heal. I had so much trauma, and I was so used to living in danger from a child and not having my needs and desires met. I was just shut down from my true inner feelings. Through all these years of his nonsense, I was totally sick of Paul in many ways. There were many good times and lots of trips and family parties and holidays. I started taking lots of classes in different creative practices like art and painting and photo darkroom. I just was really improving myself in any way I could.

One of my dear cousins, Donnie, worked in the restaurant industry. And he would come pick me up after work. And sometimes we would go hang out after with his bosses and friends, or we would go out to eat Chinese food at 1 a.m. in the morning. We always had a great time. I really had this kind of secret life from Paul rather than break up with him. He also had a very secret life from me. Even though we were in this dysfunctional relationship, I had my eye on what I wanted for my life. I didn't just like lay down and let him beat me. Deep down, I think I always knew things would have to change. I was just scared. One of the times I broke up with him, he tried to run me over with the car.

My cousin lived with his mom, my Aunt Teresa. And sometimes I would go there to wait for Donnie to come home. I would sit there and watch TV and help her fold clothes. I always felt very safe and loved by my family. I loved being with them. All this kept me very busy, and I was only seeing Paul a few nights a week and weekends.

Paul and I both loved doing a lot of the same things and often planned fun stuff. We both loved theater and getting dressed to the max to go fine dining. We would go back and forth to New York sometimes for a week for one of our birthdays.

One time, my boss suggested Paul and I go to the Pocono Mountains for a change of scenery. They had a Valentine's Day special. I should have known better because she was a little cheesy. I was so appalled when I got there with those red flocked wallpaper and the heart shaped bed. The room even had a jacuzzi. I threatened to leave until they gave us a more modern room, and when I go off, people react. I am always known for getting a major upgrade when I don't like the space, and this place was awful to my sense of aesthetics. So, I had the little cart come and get us and I shot my mouth off. We wound up getting a huge room with a private pool that was gorgeous. Paul and I were not skiers, and we were not used to the tacky entertainment in the Pocono Mountains.

We had promised that weekend to go see my father in prison because he was up that way. We both ended up getting sick with a really bad cold so we could not go to see him. Oddly, he was able to get in touch with me, somehow managing to call the hotel room. He was very upset that we weren't coming to visit him. He could get in touch with you if you were in the Himalayas if he wanted. His connections were far reaching.

I still don't like going to the mountains. I actually hate it most times unless it's in California. We both hated it. We continued going back to New York, California, the islands, and Puerto Rico where we were always by the ocean and far away from anywhere and anyone we knew.

While my father was still in prison, Paul ended up getting shot and here is where it really got tricky. But this was classic. Paul got shot around midnight. By the time we got to the hospital, it was about 12:30 a.m. His brother and father came to the hospital, but his mom was sick in bed, which was the norm for her. We stayed there all night. I went home at 7:00 a.m. in the morning to get ready for work. Yes, back in those days we were taught you never missed a Saturday in the hair business. About 9:00 a.m., when Paul opened his eyes at the hospital, there was a gilded Tower of Godiva chocolate on his table from my dad in prison.

The person who shot Paul was never caught. I still don't know who did it and at that point, I was sick of the whole scene from all that happened with my father sending the chocolate. But there were several shots fired and some hit his front door. One bullet hit the next-door neighbors because the doors were side by side. The cops came around to make their reports and everything that they needed to do, but no one was ever caught. They got him in the shoulder, and he almost lost his arm. He had many more doctors and specialist visit him. He had to wear a Tens unit which stimulates the arm and produces electric impulses that help heal the arm. It was all very shaky. We didn't know who had done this to him and why and if his arm would ever be better. He wore a sling and a cast and spent a lot of time going back and forth to doctors' offices. At that point, I began to have a much better idea of what I wanted, and some of the things I needed. I had already started exercising, had stopped smoking, and started to lose weight. I had already lost 90 lbs. in Weight Watchers.

The thing was that Paul was not always like this. I knew him from the time we were little kids. When we were young, my grandmother and his mom would take us to the movies, and they would pack bags of meatballs and sausage sandwiches and other food. We all had a great time at the movies. Paul was always doing things to make me laugh. There were the times, when we got a little older, that we could walk to Woolworths on Broad Street by ourselves. Paul and I would go there for the ice cream special. They ran a promotion where you popped a balloon to win a discounted banana split. Paul always treated me. He would pay for us to buy flowers for Mother's Day for our moms at Woolworths too. He always made me laugh. Paul was a very mischievous young boy, and he was kind to me so it made sense that we would eventually date. I knew him my whole life.

Abuse was a part of my life, and I don't think I realized that it was unacceptable in the beginning. It was part of my household and the way some of my family members behaved. My grandfather was abusive and yet he never really hurt my grandmother like Paul went after me. My grandfather could be mean in other ways, and he wouldn't allow me to go to my other grandparents. On the weekends, I would have my little suitcase packed and was so excited to be going. He would go into a rage and talk about how they never contributed any money. This would make me hysterical and cry. I would get so anxious, and I would hope my other grand-father would get there before things escalated. Little by little, my dignity was being chipped away.

I allowed Paul to get away with abusing me way too much and went back to him many times. Having experienced so much abuse as a child, it felt familiar. Unfortunately, many who have been abused, especially women, will understand how hard it is to remove your-self from an abusive relationship when your self-worth has been eroded over the years. You don't really think about it, and at that point I didn't really understand his addictions, *and my addiction was that I THOUGHT I could control it, and it would go away, or that it was something I was doing.* It's a combination of all those things, like, *it's more my fault, too.* But women who are abused ver-bally, mentally, or physically, from very young, get numb to it. *Oh well, you know, he's a good guy. He's always really sweet. He actu-ally isn't a bad person.* Paul wasn't a bad person. He was a broken person, pretending to be someone he wasn't and having all kinds of problems with his sexuality and stuffing things down. He was holding on to so much stuff that he was taking it out on me. I think he had a death wish. He wasn't in love with the guys he was picking up. They were straight men he was propositioning and a few of the men were people I had dated or had crushes on.

After I found out what he was doing, I felt like he was compet-ing with me. He picked guys that were very manly and rough. He probably wanted to feel, to some degree, submissive to them. He kept making himself a victim. That felt very sick and twisted. He was looking for some sort of validation there to be physically hurt while he was having sex. One time it hit me that after we would have these big fights, he would want to have sex with me, as if the fighting made him more sexual. I learned that was part of the con-trol and started to recognize the pattern, and it made me cringe, I really don't know why he was doing any of it because when I threatened to leave, he would go crazy. You can't really figure out crazy.

Paul was totally abused as a child by his parents. His mother would hit him even as an adult. He perpetuated what he knew. Anyone might judge me for staying so long and going back to the abuse so many times. Most people in my life had no clue what was happening to me. Eventually, when they found out, they would ask me why I kept putting up with him. I didn't know then. When I started to understand my own addiction to the drama and fighting followed by the gifts, it all made sense. Maybe I didn't think I deserved better because it was a frequent occurrence in my life. Abuse was just part of the game, part of the way for some of the women in my family who were expected to behave a certain way. A few of my grandfather's sisters were getting beaten up by their husbands too, so I watched everybody take it. I witnessed a lot of abuse in my life. It was normalized and I was surrounded by it; even just the threat of it. They normalized abuse, and it led to years of my life living in it. I hated it, and I knew to change one thing meant a whole lot was going to be changing.

It's telling though, that on the night I was getting beat up so badly by Paul, I was on the corner of Ninth and Mifflin by Southwark school. My dad's house was only a quarter of a block down the street, but I ran into the neighbor's house instead. I was able to free myself from him and get out of the car and run to the neighbors because that was safer than going to my own father. My father would have killed him right there, and I could not bear witness to that. The thing is, I'm proud of myself because now I know how to look back at all this and tell my story without the shame that I felt most of my life.

A Surprise Meeting with My Childhood Crush, Frankie Brocco

A lot of what guided me in my life, friendships and decision-making came from me working the 12-step programs of Al-Anon and Overeaters Anonymous. Al-Anon is for family and friends of anyone whose life is or was affected by alcoholism or any kind of ad-diction. That was the first program that I worked the steps and still do. It has guiding principles and steps that changed my whole life and still does. No one is perfect, certainly not me. And sometimes I could easily fall into my old ways. Al-Anon helped me make de-cisions that changed my life and pulled me out of the craziness. It opened me up to a whole new world of people who speak my lan-guage and understand the effects of a life of addiction and living with addicts. I also had to conquer my own behaviors that came out of dealing with addiction like jealousy, rage, controlling hab-its, and believing that I could solve everyone's problems and help everyone, even when they didn't care about it or want my help. I finally got into the program at about 30 years of age. Overeaters Anonymous is for anyone affected by the use of food in any way—overeating, undereating, binging, vomiting, or depriving. And for me, it has been a lifelong struggle of working the steps, having a sponsor or sponsees and sometimes multiple sponsors. My eating disorder has subsided by working my program and several other things that I will write and talk about hopefully in my next book.

There was a time when I just couldn't stand my life anymore, prob-ably after a beating from Paul at 28. Even though I was overweight, I always tried to look great and do my hair and makeup and have beautiful clothes made for me. I made an appointment at Hall Mercer Mental Health Center, a part of Pennsylvania Hospital, which is still a wonderful place if you need help with therapy, and if you can't afford it, they prorate you. One day when I went there, I was so forlorn that when I got to the desk and was told I missed my appointment, I just broke down sobbing, scared to death of Paul and what I needed to do. They gave me another appointment a week after that and that helped.

As I walked out, there was a hot dog stand and sandwich cart, and Oh my God! who was standing right there but Frankie B. He owned a bunch of similar carts all over the city and just happened to be stopping to check on that one as I walking out of the door of the hospital. We looked at each other, and I wasn't sure if he recognized me. But he did, and we gave each other the biggest hug. I pushed my total embarrassment to the side. I was too much of a mess to feel or know what my heart was telling me. That came later. He asked me how I was doing. I'm sure he could see my mascara smeared and my puffy eyes. I was so embarrassed about my weight. If I were 160 pounds thinner, the whole scene maybe would have been different. I did not feel like I deserved love or that anyone could love me at that weight. I guess that my life went the way it was meant to be. My brother was always friends with Frankie and his son. So, over the years I would hear how he asked for me. I can still feel the young love I felt for him from grade school and think how if I could write this story differently, what it could have been. But once when I saw him as a teenager, I could see how he was happy, and I felt how the girl he married was perfect for him and how much he loved her. I think they remained married until he died. I was so happy for him.

So, that day we talked for a while and he introduced me to this kid working for him and told him if I ever wanted to buy something from the cart, to just give it to me free of charge. It was that way in South Philly a lot. If I was somewhere and someone knew me either for myself or my family, I got things for free, like John's Water Ice, the best in the city. To this day, when I go home, I always go to my favorite places and many times I will see the sons of the people I knew who own the restaurants now and for several reasons, I don't say who I am. Some don't know me, their dads and my dad were connected, but I'm never sure if it was in a good way or not. Lots of times I just don't feel like talking about my dad or my brother, and I don't want them to think I expect anything. With Bunny, everywhere we went, she made it known. Also, I really wasn't proud of the idea that they may have known my dad because of his business dealings with them, and I really didn't want to be associated with anything he did. I always felt that way. I'd rather be associated with my grandfather and our own family than my dad. And as I got older, I wanted to be known for me and not my father. And yet, I wanted people to know that I was a badass and that if they fucked with me, they were going to get it back in spades. I have changed immensely and when I feel that coming on, I breathe, I pray, and I tell myself I'm not in South Philly anymore or even Center City.

I still think of Frankie B. fondly, even though he is dead now. He and my brother tried to call me after I moved to Atlanta. What came through was a Philly number at like 1:00 a.m. I was not answering that phone. I was in love with Lynn, and we were sound asleep in bed. No way was I getting involved with Philly stuff. I missed out because I later found out that he and my brother were at some bar and Frankie said, "Call your sister." He told my brother he wanted to tell me how much he loved me when we were young and how he always loved me. I finally had some closure around our young love.

I never felt the need to see a medium or psychic until I came home one day many years after running into him, and I felt Frankie's spirit in my new house. I was floored and scared. This has happened to me over the years, and I never realized how psychic I was. Psycho, yes, but this was a whole other story. In later years, I was living in this big house and had just finished with most of the renovations, and I felt this spirit and I just knew it was Frankie. I called my friend, and she asked me if I had a picture of him and I remembered that I did from grade school. I did what she said and made a little space on my altar. I felt him directing me around the house to my computer. There were more nights where I felt him directing me around the house. It took me several years, and an excellent psychic who I still use, but Frankie came through loud and clear.

The psychic would tell me some things I couldn't put together. She said that Frankie had always loved me thin or fat and that was very healing for me. My sister and my good friend, Rae Rae, remembered a lot of things that kept coming up like the way he always followed me around like a puppy dog. I learned that I pushed him away for several reasons. The main reason was not feeling worthy because of my weight. I wanted the little jerk offs to stop singing that Tessie and Frankie were lovers. Many years later, I can still feel the pain of regret that I was too young to know how to handle it. I am still so grateful for the times we met each other at his hot dog stands while I was walking to and from Center City. He got to see the slim me while I was losing 160 lbs. I wish I could have heard from him or what he told my brother. I send prayers and peace to his soul.

From MAFIA PRINCESS *to* LESBIAN CHIC

CHAPTER 10

SELF HELP... HELPS!

New Career Beginnings

I was working in a salon close to Wharton and Drexel with lots of brilliant and attractive clients mostly men. I had already lost 90 pounds on Weight Watchers, but then I stopped smoking and gained 18 pounds back. When I met the guys who came to the salon for haircuts, they were all students, super smart, good looking, and successful. I was still 60 pounds overweight. I was too self-conscious and didn't have enough confidence to attempt to date any of the guys that came to us.

I felt too insecure, and Paul was fighting with me, even though I had broken up with him. One day, he got my brother—another abuser, who was always on his side—and they came to my work to confront me. The salon was in this complex at RiverLoft Condos that used to be an old clothing factory, with steps that went swirling up to the top floors. It was all glass, so anybody on the bottom floor could see right up. Paul and my brother came running up screaming at me. The owners stopped them before they could get in the door of the salon and told them they had called the cops. Paul and my brother ran away before the cops arrived.

While I was working at this salon, I had this client—an older, married woman. She would come to me to get her hair styled, and she saw how uncomfortable I was in my body. She was so sweet. By the time I met her, I had already lost a good bit of that weight, but I was struggling to keep that off. I can see her to this day sitting in my chair. She had six kids, and said to me, "Well, I lost over 100 pounds, and I did it through this program called Trevose Behavior Modification, and we are a study group for the University of Penn's program that has been very successful." She was lovely. I loved her. I really connected a lot with her. Older women made me have a sense that they were worth listening to. Maybe it's because my grandmothers raised me, mostly, and they always seemed to have words of wisdom. She said, "I want to tell you about this program that I go to that offers behavior modification. I think it might help you. I want to invite you to come along sometime." And I did go, and I joined the program, and I lost another 70 pounds. Altogether, I lost 160 pounds, and I actually became a leader for the program. Oddly, I've always had these leader roles. Everybody wants to put me in a leader role as soon as they meet me.

I started doing water pills too because the behavior modification group was free to be part of as long as you met your monthly goal weight. Otherwise, if you missed that goal twice, you were out. I was in therapy at that point, but I was struggling to keep the weight off, thus the pills.

The owners from the RiverLoft moved and opened up a salon on 21st and Samson St. We expanded the basement as well so I could do hair for younger people, because upstairs was mostly older women. I loved these older Jewish women. They taught me so much and a lot of my clientele at that point was Jewish. They were role models for me. I loved how they bragged about their kids and families. I loved that they belonged to the Hadassah organization and admired all the good they did locally and in the world. So, that showed me a whole different life than my family that was always complaining. I'm sure there were Italians that bragged about their kids, but that wasn't us. I was thin as a rail. I wore all these high fashion clothes, and at that point, I looked stunning. I got many accolades for my looks. Everywhere I went, everybody was telling me how beautiful I looked. And finally, some of my clients were like, "Oh my God, look at you. Look at you!!! You need to be in New York. You need to be working at a high-end New York salon." There were a lot of Jewish ladies coming to us then when I lost my weight. Everybody was saying, "Go to New York," because I was always in New York. I did interview in New York, but it really wasn't for me. It just was too, too much and far from my family.

I lost 160 pounds, and my mother never said a word. Well, there was hardly any praise for anything in that house. I'll tell you what she used to do though. Every night I would be eating. I would eat and eat because I was looking for love. She would be upstairs in her own world and then she'd come down after she slept to eat some dinner finally. And she would say, "Look at you. How can you eat like that? How can you eat so much food like that?" She never said words of love. One day I ran into one of her friends at the salon and she told me, "Oh, your mother talks about you all the time. How wonderful you are and how you take her everywhere, and how you lost so much weight." Wow! That floored me. She hardly ever said a word to me to encourage me or show me love but told other people how great I am. Today, it touches me when I see parents being sweet with their kids. It's definitely something I missed out on growing up and something I try to do with my godchildren.

I was outgrowing my current salon, and the owner knew it. She expanded the salon downstairs to cater to a hipper crowd, and we hired this girl, Chris. She was very different than I am, white as could be and androgynous. She was kind of like a Cyndi Lauper meets Boy George type with her head half shaved and all that, but she cut hair exquisitely. I was still just doing my styling and haircuts based on the training I previously had and started repping a color line and teaching advanced techniques at other salons. I hadn't gone to any of the big schools where they did more advanced training. I went to an academy, but there you learn basic styles and so, while I was still a great haircutter, when I saw the way she clipper cut, that was the key. At that point in time, it was all about unisex, and men were coming in, and girls too, and I did not know how to cut like she cut. So, that was the beginning of me realizing that I needed to change. She told me that she had gone to England to learn how to cut at an exclusive school. I thought, *oh, God, I gotta do something here.* I was always going to classes. I've always continued to educate myself, even to this day so I knew I had to make some changes. One thing I had going for me regardless was my salesmanship. When we had contests, the other stylists thought they were going to beat me, but they wouldn't because I was a very good salesperson. I still am a very good salesperson. Now I knew I had to add more techniques to my repertoire and move upwards in my career. I was now motivated.

Regaining Dignity and Self-Worth

My self-help journey has been a long road. I started Al-Anon first because Paul an alcoholic. I had gotten up to 308 pounds (and I am not a very tall woman, about five foot four,) and even though I always looked beautiful, I never had the self-worth I should have. I even had my clothes custom made. Paul used to call me his Diana Ross.

When I decided, *I'm gonna lose this weight,* going to Weight Watcher's, my mom, my aunt, my bestie Debbie, a whole bunch of us joined together. But as a funny aside, we would go to the Melrose Diner after we got weighed at the meetings, of course.

I was still living at home as I was losing the weight, but I had reached a standstill. The woman I admired, Lil Berman, who got me into the weight loss program had a nice group going when we moved it to Center City. We would go out to eat together as a group and learn how to do things like split an appetizer or even entrees and chose healthier menu items, creating better habits.

One day, she said to me, "You know what? You're not going to be able to get this weight off and keep it off until you move out of your grandparents' house." "Oh, wow!" I cried when she said that. I saw that she had a point. I was very comfortable there in my own way, because I could go between the two grandparents when I wanted to get away from either of them. It was the best of all worlds.

I did move out. And my grandfather was furious. I was only moving in the new duplex across the street and three houses down from my aunt Marian and still surrounded by family on all sides. I lived so close that when Paul and I broke up, my golden retriever would go and wake my grandmother up when I came home at two or three in the morning after dancing. That's how close the houses were. And my grandfather made a big deal out of my moving because he thought I was doing it because I lost all this weight. He figured now I was going to have all kind of men come up there. My Uncle Joe knew that that wasn't me. He might have set my grandfather straight, but he didn't!

I liked who I was after losing the weight. I loved the way I looked and all of the advantages that came with being seen as skinny, hot, and beautiful. I loved food in general but of course, Italian food, bread, and definitely carbs have been my poison of choice. I was finally beginning to learn how to match inside with how I looked outside. Even though I looked fantastic outside, inside, the same old nagging feelings of not being good enough, low self-worth, were lurking in my head and I was a little scared in my new body.

South Street, The Hippest Street in Town

I began to see the transformation on South Street which was where everybody went to hang out. It started to look like Greenwich village. As each bridal store closed, all kinds of wonderful shops and cool restaurants started opening. It was a fun place. Later, the hippies all came in and took over South Street. But at the time I worked there, there was a store called Garland of Letters. It was two doors down from my job, and I started going in there and reading these books. They had crystals and all kinds of pretty things. I saw a sign on their wall saying they were offering a yoga class. Yoga and meditation had already been on my horizon. I joined the class and started doing yoga. I didn't know how high level a yoga master the instructor, Dr. Pratap, was. I didn't find that out until much later about the different levels of yogis and spiritual teachers and gurus, but he was fabulous. He was the founder and director of the Sky Foundation and was the director of the yoga program at Thomas Jefferson University in Philly. He was this tiny little Indian man with long hair. They also offered Hindu studies after yoga. True yogis do yoga to calm the body in preparation for meditation. I started to take the lessons, and I connected with Hinduism and a new way of looking at my spirituality. I was always curious about different cultures, dating back to my fascination with Uncle Fred and Aunt Connie. One day, while in a particular yoga pose, he basically told me that my stomach was too big. I was like a size eight or maybe even a six at that point. Jesus! Okay! He said that my stomach was getting in the way of me doing some of the harder poses and it was true to some degree. Certain poses are very, very hard.

I stopped. I just stopped at that point, okay? I went on about my life, learning and experiencing new things and meeting new people. I ditched yoga and joined the Queen Village Racquetball Club. Paul joined with me, and I started doing all kinds of stuff there. I actually started teaching, substitute teaching, and my whole world changed. My whole world changed drastically after I lost the weight and got into a higher-level salon. That's the thing, when you lose that kind of weight, it gives you access to places you never would have been part of before. I don't care what anybody says because when I was 308 pounds, not one of those salons that later were begging me to go to them would have given me a second look. I became president of the Philadelphia Hair Fashion Guild, and all those Italian men that ran the best salons in Philadelphia, Center City, wouldn't have looked at me for their salons before I lost the weight—even at 220 pounds.

At the Queen's Village Racquetball Club, I started working out and began hanging out with a whole different group and getting really fit. My father started remarking that my legs were too skinny. The man who criticized every part of my body was now telling me that my legs were too skinny. My grandmother who I lived with told me that I looked like I was sick. "Do you have cancer? You're too skinny." Talk about whiplash.

There was another teacher at the club, and she was beautiful. She was a dancer who taught aerobics most of the time. Sometimes a group of us would go out to lunch after classes and we would party together, too. When I could get away from Paul, we'd go out dancing. And so, my life just kept evolving, kept getting better, and better, and better. There was a guy who was in the aerobics class who was really cute, not that I was attracted to him because he looked like my family, and I could see he was gay. We were at the water fountain together and he had his face in the water. When he stood up and looked at me, I asked him, "What's your name? You look like one of my cousins, Donnie Romeo." My name is Donnie Mallace," he said. "What? I think we're related." He was my grandfather's nephew and my second cousin. I started hanging out with him and some of his friends.

Donnie was an art teacher, and he would be hired to go on cruises to teach arts and crafts on his school breaks. He got friends to fill in on cruises that he couldn't attend. I got to fill in as art director on one of the cruises and it was a blast, but I didn't have the time to do that more than once. I brought my friend Dot with me. She was an Irish girl from the other side of South Philly, but she was older than me and white as could be. She was precious, but she was so on the straight and narrow. She had an office job and knew nothing about arts and crafts. But we laughed our way through those classes and that cruise, and I will never forget it. I was broken up from Paul at the time and told Dot that I had been with him for so long that I didn't remember how to date. She was hysterical. The ship was the Leonardo da Vinci, and all the crew was Italian. I started flirting the moment I got on the ship and the gorgeous men were flirting back. I had so many dates that week that I couldn't keep up.

CHAPTER 11

MOVING ON UP

Once I lost all the weight, I felt good enough about myself to go after a position in one of the high-profile salons in the middle of the fashion district.

One day, I was all dressed up and I went for a walk. I went to get my nails done and the salon next door looked like a cool place. It had a sign in their window *looking for a stylist*. All the people in the Richard Nicholas Hair Studio were beautiful. A lot of the big salons hire you for different reasons. You must look a certain way. I went in and I got hired right away. The salon owner did training all the time, and I knew this was key to my success so, I left the other salon and started there almost immediately.

When I went home and told my grandfather and my uncle Joe I was leaving *Looks Hair Salon*, they had a fit because the owner of that salon was dating one of my grandfather's friends from the Bocce club. Frankly, she had a very active sex life and slept with so many different men at the same time while she had a husband and kids. She was a very beautiful woman, and she would drink from early in the morning. She got away with it until one of her boyfriends got shot while she was entertaining another man. My grandfather said, "How can you do that to her?" "This is for my career," I told him. "What are you talking about? Your career? You cut hair. How is that a career?" "I am a hair stylist, and yes, that is my career," I said. "I want to advance." He didn't get it because nobody ever used that word when talking about cutting hair or beauty salons. My mom didn't use that word. My aunts didn't use that word.

Regardless of my family's opinion. I took the job with Richard Nicholas Hair Studio to work at a much more prestigious salon. From my first interview, I knew the owner, Nick, had his act together and a plan for his success and I wanted to be a part of that and learn from him. He blew my mind open regarding the industry and how to cut hair. So, I went to work for Nick Berardi.

My new boss, Nick, required us to look hip and fashionable yet effortless. Being a South Philly girl, I really had to adjust my fashion sense and play it down. He wanted the image of our clients and stylists to be stylish without seeming to try. We did haircuts with strong shapes and added color as a complement, very Sassoon-like. All the stylists had their own look, but it was what I would call, Street Style Chic, which includes casual and chic elements often mixing high-end fashion with vintage looks. We were encouraged to show individuality but stay in keeping with this modern approach to fashion.

My life at that time was full of change in every area, and I was excited about my new direction and filled with hope. All the hard work I was doing felt so gratifying and was paying off. Working at a premier salon taking classes every week with Nick who was a Vidal-Sassoon-trained teacher was incredible. I learned how to cut hair in a totally different way. Nick was an incredible educator. We had to be at workshops and classes every week at the salon. He didn't care what you had going on. You had to start at a certain time and learn how to cut and learn how to stand properly. He threw my shoes away once because he didn't think they were suitable.

I didn't know my identity yet. For example, my mom had this very pretty dress that I always liked on her, and I wore it to work one day. I had these beige pumps I thought paired well with the dress. "Are you coming to work today to meet a doctor or a lawyer?" he snarked at me when he saw what I was wearing. I looked at him, but then I got it. I didn't look hip enough. All the other girls were wearing clothes from these famous boutiques right around the area. I worked in that outfit that day, but that led me to finally find my identity in fashion. Another day, I came in and I had a big scarf around my head. I thought it was very fashionable. Our receptionist, who was a bitch, and eventually ended up getting caught stealing, said, "You better not let Nick see that that scarf on your head. He's going to have a fit." While I understood his business objective, his criticisms of me felt too close to home, and I started getting anxiety attacks. I was attending Behavior Modification program meetings in Trevose, northeast of Philly. I had to drive there because it was so far from my house that I couldn't get there by bus. I couldn't drive on the highway and had to take the back roads which made the trip even longer— two hours to get there at night.

Nick was the one who told me that I needed to go to Vidal Sassoon in England. But I went to school in Toronto instead. I started helping him with the Philadelphia Hair Fashion Guild. Nick was the president of the board and was making the decisions of who he wanted to bring in. The guild met nine months out of the year, and each month we brought in a new, famous artist, sometimes from Italy, sometimes from France. Once we actually had Barbara Streisand's hairdresser, Jon Peters' business partner come. We had very famous people come. The Philadelphia Hair Fashion Guild members were the top salon owners in Center City, mostly all Italian men. Each year, I moved up and did things to assist. I picked the restaurants where we took the guests, helped coordinate schedules, and made sure things went smoothly.

I eventually ended up becoming the president of the organization many years later. With my goals in place, I started assisting Nick and dealing with these famous people that came to Philadelphia. We had hairdressers, educators, and salon owners from all over the world, including people like Vidal Sassoon, Aveda's founder, Horst, Gino from Boston. I would do the backup work. I would volunteer my time to do the shampooing or apply the chemicals. One time, I actually did this perm that was my own idea, a variation on how we were doing perms. All these people at the show were hair artists who I idolized over the years. They asked me, "How did you do that perm?" I was so proud of my work and their comments on what I was doing.

This was the beginning of how I got to the top. Working at Richard Nichols, opened my world, as well as all the people that came in there. The women I worked with were striking. One woman, Sheika, looked like she walked off the cover of a Chanel magazine. Nick would laugh and say, "If you two could share one brain." For example, I did his color for him in the beginning, but he didn't always like the way I did color. He liked the way Sheika did color differently. He liked the way I did perms, and he liked different things about each of our talents. "If you could be one person, you would be the most perfect hairdresser in the world," Nick would tell us. She was really stunning, stylish, and tiny.

There were so many interesting people around and my clientele was changing rapidly. I always had an attraction to women off and on, but I was still with Paul. Some of my friends were catching on. And then there was this international entertainment attorney and her business partner who started coming to me for hair styling. All I can say is, I realized my attraction one day as I was fixing my makeup before she came in. I felt the rush of excitement. We developed a nice relationship and whenever we were together, we couldn't stop laughing. I became more aware of my sexuality. I always had crushes on people of color or different ethnic groups. Also, at that time, I broke up with Paul and I left South Philly and moved three miles to Center City. You might think I was moving to a different continent the way my family reacted.

All these changes that were happening felt great and fabulous, and yet I was still scared about them. Moving into Center City was a big deal for me even though it was only three miles away. And every Monday, I would walk home to see my family, stop at the Italian Market, pick up provisions for everyone, and spend my day there.

Criminally Sophisticated

Dad worked in a Country Club on the Main Line when he was younger, and he really liked the fine art of cooking and serving food in upscale establishments. He made the best Caesar salad ever, and he loved flambéing desserts and preparing food tableside. He passed that on to me. I got used to going to very special places to dine with my dad and his family. He taught me how to move in high-end circles. One time, Bunny went and told my dad that I was acting like a Jewish Princess. Not an Italian Princess, because now that I was in my 20s, I was setting my own standards of how I wanted to be and what I would put up with.

I liked all the great restaurants in Philly, Jersey, and wherever we went. I was just as comfortable there as I was at Nick's Roast Beef. I was as comfortable walking into a room of executives at the Ritz Carlton as I was walking into the Bocce Club. Maybe more so because I didn't have to dodge bullets. One of my favorite Italian restaurants to this day is Dante and Luigi's. Years ago, there was a big hit, and someone got killed. I often went there with Bunny for dinner. We were seated at the table next to some of the big guys. We just minded our own business and was very respectful of their space. Bunny and I were too busy having our own fun.

I loved making the transition into the high world of fashion and helping my boss Nick wine and dine famous artists from all over the world who came to teach us. It was easy for me with my background. I liked going to conferences in New York, sitting with some of the owners and stylists from big top name companies. I also learned how to listen and not open my mouth—which is a rarity for me—when conversations didn't apply to me. But I was listening to every word to learn about the industry, just like the curious little girl I always was. I still feel that way. So much to learn and so little time. I also always try to sit in the front row at classes and conferences. I wanted to learn as much as I could. I asked lots of questions, which I was told most of the time were very good. I just wanted to grow and fill up with all this knowledge. I have always taken extra classes, workshops, college courses, and God-willing, I will do this to the day I leave planet Earth. I already planned some of the classes I want to take next to further my writing career.

Elevating My Craft

Nick did not want a makeup counter in the salon, and I really missed that. After about four years, I realized I was missing some of the aspects of my career. When an opportunity presented itself, I went to a salon in the Bellevue Stratford Hotel, The Pierre and Carlo de Roma. It was one of the top salons in the city for years, and it was a totally different atmosphere. It was beautiful and looked like a Roman villa. While working for Nick was of a modern, hip salon, for both men and women, this new salon was more of a European salon. They were from Italy, and it was amazing. They were known all over the world, and they introduced me to things that I didn't know about. They told us that we had to go to France to study. They were all about going to Paris twice a year. I couldn't afford to go twice a year, but I did go, and it was amazing. They paid for the schooling but not the trip part.

At my new salon the dress code was very different. We were not allowed to wear pants. We had to dress like we were going to the opera. I would go in with like a tux top, sometimes in frilly skirts, looking like Madonna. After work, there were all parties at night, people throwing fancy cocktail parties. So, I started going to them, and there was all this incredible food. I never drank a lot; one, two drinks back then were enough for me, but the food was amazing. So, I start putting the weight on. And when I went to get weighed every month, I would think, *what the hell am I going to do?* I don't want to get kicked out of the program, so I had to find other ways to lose the weight before the monthly weigh-in. I was already taking water pills, but then I moved onto laxatives.

At that point, I worked a 20-minute walk home through Rittenhouse Square, which was lovely. I got to know more of the people around there, shop and boutique owners, artists, and all. A few of my former clients who became besties lived in that area too and that solidified our friendships. Walking through the maze of shops and restaurants was fun. And now that I had been in 12-step programs and met so many more people who became my best friends through life and their children became my godchildren. My whole life and the things I wanted and the people I wanted to be with were all right there. I remained very close to my family and merged my worlds. I had a new sense of freedom and urgency to embrace life.

While I was moving upwards in my life and my career, my sister Sadie was now on her second husband. Her first was divine and I loved him a lot and I was also somewhat jealous and yet super happy for her. But my sister, being who she was, met a guy in California who was an Italian lawyer who didn't speak English, and she couldn't speak Italian. I could write a whole book about my sister's antics. There were many times I wanted to beat her up and a few times I did and yes, I've made many amends. I love her very much.

So, while she's off to Italy—she had already lived in Florida, California and who knows where else—and with my dad in jail, a lot of the responsibility of my two Agnes grandparents was on me. I have always had a lot of energy and was able to handle a lot. Paul was out of the picture and the breakup was not easy. We both came out of it alive. That's what I was hoping for. It could've happened a lot sooner, but I'm sure he would have been killed. Even though my dad was in jail through a lot of the years, it would've just taken a phone call to the prison and Paul could have been dead. I could never do that! I just couldn't plus that's the last thing I ever wanted on my conscience. I already had such guilt and shame about my life.

My brother was around and moved back in with my mom and grandparents. It always bothered me that this cute, sweet baby brother that I loved so much became an asshole and a monster at times. Especially when he was on meth. Louis was really stuck. My father never did anything to help him. He was a great artist from a child, but once again, no one got that except my grandfather's brother, Joe. He helped get Louis a scholarship to The Academy of Fine Arts. The school was amazing with ties to lots of famous artists around the world. For me, it was so heartbreaking to watch his life play out. He tried to act life a tough guy to live up to Dad's expectations, but Louis was not like that. He was a softie, and an artist, and my Uncle Joe was teaching him how to box. He became violent when he was on meth, and I had to run from him once when he flipped me over a TV. That was the only time he ever hit me, and I ran next door to my Uncle Joe's. And somehow, he never touched me again. He was angry at me my whole life, and we had this on and off relationship, but then sometimes he could be so sweet.

Pierre and Carlo were members of *Intercoiffure Mondial*, a prestigious, international hairdressing organization dating back to 1925. Intercoiffure was established in Germany, moved to Paris after the war, and the first chapter in the US was started in Philadelphia. This professional association connected only the best salon owners in the world. Nick was also a member. I was very happy to be again in an Intercoiffure salon working with these incredible artists. This was the start of a whole new chapter and a big contributing factor in all my moves forward.

I was in love with my career because I was meeting these famous people that you only saw in major magazine and film publications. Some of the most beautiful people around were in and out of the salons that I worked at. I continued to assist with the Guild and later I became President of the Board.

Even though I changed salons, Nick and I got to work on different projects. I was already an instructor even before I went to work for Nick. I worked for Sebastian hair color line as their Creative Color Artist. I went to other salons to teach people color techniques. While at the Bellevue for more than six years, I became an educator there as well. I helped train the assistants. I also did color work using the Allegretti color line. I loved both the creative and teaching aspects at this time. It also helped me in building my self-worth.

There were several owners that were part of the Philadelphia Hair Fashion Guild that did not believe that you should have makeup in a hair salon. I have always done makeup as well as hair so, when I went to Pierre and Carlo, we had a spa, and we did makeup. When they saw how good I was at doing makeup, they wanted me to continue doing so. I did make-up for competitions, many fashion shoots, and professional videos. They even sent me to school to learn makeup tattooing. I didn't enjoy working so close to the eye or with needles and decided that tattooing wasn't for me, but I did continue to do traditional make-up at the salon and for shows.

There was a big event that my boss, Joseph, put me in charge of and suggested I partner with Nick. We put on a big event to raise money for homeless women and children. I had already been doing service for years, donating money to Women's Way and Women Against Abuse. This event was held at the Bellevue, and we built our team from salon owners in Center City, top hairdressers, and some assistants. We gave haircuts for $25 to friends and family of our own clients and that money went to the charity. It was very cathartic to work on this event, and I loved the way my life was shaping up. Professionally, my life was ascending, but personally, I was still dealing with the aftereffects of my abusive relationship and my dad in prison, and he was still busting my chops from prison.

CHAPTER 12

LONG RANGE EFFECTS
OF A CRIMINAL DAD

T he word mafia was never really said in our family. I knew better than to say it. Army was the word. And what has always irritated me is when I meet people and tell them I'm Italian, and they quietly say, "Oh, is your family in the mob?" Right then, I want to punch them in the face or ask them if they need someone whacked. Some of the mob lived in my neighborhood and all over South Philly, and my dad was a criminal associated with the mob. Since I started practicing meditation, I always say I'm five breaths away from punching someone. I'm going to say this right now. When you live across the street from people who share their food with you, and we share our food with them, even if you have a beef with them, we are still family. I went to school with a lot of the children of these people. I knew them from when they were little. My little sister and their youngest brother got caught in the park taking their clothes off at five-years-old and knowing it was just a state of innocence, I didn't think anything of it. My heart still breaks for them.

One memory that I can still feel the pain in my body from happened in the early 1980s when the Philly mob wars were on. All the old bosses were getting shot. I was walking home from South Street, and I thought I would stop by the Bocce Club to give my grandfather a hug and kiss. As I was approaching, I saw our old neighbor who, as wild as he was, I still liked him a lot. What was weird was that his head was hanging at an odd angle. I ran to the car parked right in front of the Bocce club and started hollering "Johnny, Johnny." It was freezing out and I could see his breath, but he didn't move. So, I started banging on the car window where his head was leaning. I didn't see any blood or anything. Finally, he woke up and looked at me. I think he either was exhausted or drunk or who knows what. But I explained how scared I was that I thought he was dead. I really cared about this man and his family. They lived across from us. The pain for me was deep, although I never said a word. Growing up in South Philly, we knew about the code of ethics—omerta—that were the rules they lived by. In reality, most of us lived by that code, including my criminal dad who never ratted anyone out and consequently spent a lot of time in jail.

The cost of having a criminal dad is brutal. It affects everyone differently. It affects the family and not just the immediate family. It reverberates and hurts so many layers of people. My father was so charming and conniving. He was younger than the older made men and yet he was feared by so many people because he didn't follow the rules of the "Army."

He would threaten people, and I don't think he really had to answer to anyone. The older mob had a set of standards, but my dad did not want to adhere to them. The older guys did not want drugs being sold, but my dad was the one bringing them in. He wasn't in a position that required him to follow those rules, instead, he danced around the outside of their inner circle and forged his own path which generally led him to his own troubles and often in prison. And he was a thief as well. For instance, one of his many crimes happened when I was in my 20s.

He sold a large amount of drugs to some college students in Center City. What did the idiot do that he thought was so brilliant? He got dressed up as a cop, and he and his buddies who were actual cops went back to the apartment on a "drug bust." They took all the drugs back from the students, so now they had the money and the drugs to sell again to some other suckers, I assume. The students called the police station, confused as to whether or not they were in some kind of trouble and to say that cops had raided their apartment only to find out that there was no record of any busts. The students picked my dad out from mug shots.

This led to an investigation of the dirty cops and, of course, my father. Soon, there they all were across the front page of the newspaper, showing my father wearing a full cop uniform and hat. They thought they were so clever, but they all had to serve prison time. Dad was in jail for at least four more years for that little episode. They had to be high on coke.

So, once again, trials, and I was just sick of it and gave up. I had no intention to help save him. He would call me from jail to tell me how he was doing. He would get my hopes up telling me that he was working out, lifting weights and jogging, and then he would pop that illusion, saying, "There's a few guys that I have to take care of when I get out." It was like a knife to my heart. He'd say shit like this, so I held such fear inside of me. I remember feeling numb.

The other thing that drove me nuts was he put my grandparents and all of us in precarious situations. But, of course, his parents were always finding people, whether it be judges or councilmen and whoever else they could get to intervene. He was always trying to find people who would drive my grandmother to see him in prison. This time, he connected my grandmother with the wife of one of the cops he got into trouble with. Those two became "buddy buddy." He did this kind of shit all the time. He always found a way to entangle my grandparents with these people so that they could help him while he was in jail. He was always working every angle that he could to his benefit. One of the cop's wives worked in a nursing home. My grandmother, Susie Q, suddenly wanted to leave my grandfather. At this point, my grandparents were both in their early 60s. My grandmother took a job at this cockroach-ridden and disgusting nursing home where they gave her a little apartment. At first, she told no one where she was until finally, she called me.

My grandfather was so pathetic. He sat night and day crying his eyes out on the couch. I felt so bad for him. My father, his son, was serving time and now his wife had taken off. I was afraid if I told my grandfather that I knew where she was, he would go kill my grandmother or hurt her. He wasn't the hitting type or violent, but he was so full of pent-up rage from his own childhood and that his father had committed suicide, I thought it was better to not mess with him. My heart still hurts when I think of it. He was sobbing so much, and one night he said to me, "Elaine, I never wanted to tell you this, but your grandmother wanted to try for a girl, but we had the two boys, and I didn't want any more kids, so I refused to try. She would not have sex with me anymore after you were born. You were the girl she wanted." He was just sobbing and sobbing and sobbing. I would sleep there because I had my room there and was going back and forth between the two households. I stayed to make sure he was okay and to do whatever I could to bring him some peace.

At one point, his sister-in-law yelled at me in a very cocky way in Red's Hoagies, which was a very famous shop on the corner of ninth and Mifflin where people would line up and buy boxes of hoagies. There she was, standing as tall as could be with her wild hair and big mouth. Of course, I was always taught respect, and I did like her well enough, but that day, she just went at me in the front of the store at the checkout. I remember her saying, "Elaine, you know where your grandmother is. She would never leave without you knowing it. Why are you letting your grandfather suffer like that?" I was suffering too. I was trying to be very respectful to her because she was my aunt and I loved her husband Uncle Victor, my grandfather Tony's brother, and the place was packed. I really don't know how I, with my big mouth, held my composure. "Think what you want," I replied. And when she walked out of the store she said, "You're a fucking liar." As I was paying my bill, I said to one of the brothers who owned the place, "She's an idiot," and I left. Of course she was right! I knew!

Eventually, after a few months of this nonsense, she went back to my grandfather. He was crying when she came into the house, but she wasn't crying. She returned not so much because she missed him or wanted to come home was because it was a high-end nursing home where she actually saw them strip people when they died of all their jewelry and belongings, and she saw so much mistreatment of these old people. I was with Paul at the time, and we took her back home. We stayed a while to make sure things were peaceful. After that, she never left again until she died.

I was sick of the shenanigans and chaos and being thrust in the middle of everything all the time. I didn't ask for any of this. I felt responsible for taking care of everyone's feelings, and it was exhausting. Meanwhile, I wasn't fully aware of the depth of my pain and anger. I hid it with comedic relief and food. Losing weight is so much more than about the food. Yes, it is also about proper nutrition and exercise, but under my top weight of 310 lbs. were layers and layers of tears, trauma, fear, anger, resentment, and most of all, shame. I wasn't yet aware that feelings of joy, my sexuality, and freedom were possible for me. There's a lot that I couldn't let out because they shamed me about everything and anything. I didn't have the best life, and yet I made the best life of what was available.

For instance, I always wanted to have children and from that very first punch from Paul, that ended that. I chose (I'm not sure if I did the actual choosing) not to have children. Even as I got more recovery, the fear was so ingrained in me for many reasons, above all the fear of what my father would or could do to my own kids given any time around them. He stole me, kidnapped me for a few days when I was a baby, driving everybody crazy. Would he do that with a grandchild or abuse them sexually? Of course he would, and I was not taking that chance.

And it wasn't only him. I feared of all these people that were sexually abused by family members and then my ex Paul, were absolutely fucking crazy, and so were his mother and father. I would not allow my children around anybody. I didn't trust anyone. I was so busy taking care of everyone else since I was a kid, that I was blind to my own human needs.

When I moved into Center City Philly, I really did a lot more growing up and met so many new people. My apartment was on the third floor, and I was taking a break from unpacking. I was tired, lonely, and hungry and went to visit an acquaintance I had met named Michael, who owned an Italian market in my new neighborhood. While I had a couple of friends and many clients in the area, I missed having my family nearby, so it was nice to have an Italian friend near me. I felt so comfortable talking to him. He felt like family to me.

My intentions were to flirt with him, and when we met, it seemed his intentions were aligned. He was very handsome and slim and looked like a cross between Tony Danza and John Travolta. Before you knew it, he offered to come over and cook for me at my condo. I said no, and he offered to take me out instead. When he picked me up and came in to see my place, he stopped and was admiring my jewelry that was sitting out. I thought it was unusual. We went two doors down to this local restaurant and were eating and drinking. He commented about my red lipstick on the wine glass and how sexy it was. He asked if I knew this girl, Carol, that I went to grade school with. She was a makeup artist in the area. He told me he lived with her for four years. That triggered my memory of her stories. She had crazy stories of almost every guy she lived with. We ended up back in my apartment. I was very attracted to him, and we started making out. Somewhere along the way, it was not working. When he asked me to slap him in the face, I told him I wasn't into that. That was the end of our romantic adventures, but we remained loyal friends for many years. When I talked to Carol, she was surprised I didn't know about Michael/Michelle. She came home one time to find him in a wig and her makeup and clothes. She said, "He looked better than I did!" And then I remembered that story. There were a lot more even wackier ones!

I met Pat Q at a meeting with our friend, Ellen. We started talking after our meetings and would go to get yogurt together at Skinny Delights. I really liked her personality, and I became attracted to her and those feelings initially scared me as I was just rediscovering my feelings for women. I talked to my therapist about it and that I was still attracted to men as well. She explained that there's a broad spectrum of sexuality. I realized I needed to say something to Pat to see how she felt. I was unaware that she already had a long-term partner. Pat told me that she loved me and valued our friendship. I told her that these feelings were new for me, and I wasn't sure if I could handle the friendship. We became very close and little by little were hanging out more.

Eventually, I met her partner, Sharon, at a party. Sharon was lovely and I was never one to interfere in a relationship. I met both their families and felt close to them. Pat and Sharon were and are a big part of my family. They took me into their lives and hearts. During that time, they fixed me up with several of their friends. Their friends embraced me and became my clients as well. It was fun hanging out with the Chestnut Hill and West Mount Airy crowd, and I still love them to this day!

There was a street artist, Joe, a painter, who set up on the street down from where I worked who reminded me of Bob Marley. He had dreads and smooth dark skin, and he painted beautifully. So many people would walk by and talk to him. My friend Valerie knew him, so I went by and talked to him often as well. He was very successful and intriguing, and I would think to myself, *I wonder where he hangs out.* So, one night, I went to this sushi place that

I really liked. I was by myself that night, and Joe was there. I sat right next to him at the sushi bar, and we start talking about his art and music. He used to see me coming in and out of the salon and we would say hi to one another, so he recognized me. He was very, very intriguing and good looking but somehow reminded me of my dad. When I get that feeling, I know that they're not for me. But he was cool and an artist, and I always liked that kind of crowd.

There was an article in the paper about this place called Zanzibar Blue that intrigued me because it talked about their diverse customers, their menu and live international jazz. I felt the place was fabulous from the minute I walked through the doors. They had Sade and Norah Jones music playing all the time. When you entered the front of the place, there was this gorgeous area around the bar. People were mingling, having drinks and appetizers. The owners would be out front greeting people and right away I met the owners, Benjamin and Robert. I was very attracted to their personalities, and they immediately felt like family to me. It was so cool. In a sense, it reminded me of my grandfather's Bocce club where everyone knew each other and you felt welcome. The difference was the crowd. Even though there were some other jazz clubs in Philly that we went to, this suited me perfectly from the beginning.

Zanzibar was so comfortable to me, and I loved listening to live music. When I was a little girl, my uncle would practice with his band at home, and he would sing to me while I danced. And then as little as four or five years old, my mom and one of her best friends would go to the Fort Pitt Club in Atlantic City on New York Avenue. People would come in from the beach to listen to music and get some drinks. The Unique Joyriders, my uncle's band, would do the jam sessions there on the weekends and they would bring me along. My mom and Joanie were about twenty and blonde—just two gorgeous Italians.

Wherever we went, even on the amusement park rides, the guys always let us go for free or give us extra rides. At the Fort Pitt, they let me sit on the bar so I could see my uncle and, of course, my mom and Joanie would have me dancing. I got so used to all that extra attention from my uncle and the band. When I found Zanzibar, it was like a replay from the parts that I loved from my past.

I think it was the coolest place ever in Philly. The people who went there were a very sophisticated crowd with a lot of diversity; many highly artistic and educated and accomplished beautiful people from across the city at that time. It was a real melting pot of people representing different ethnic backgrounds and cultures and offering an upscale experience. I got to know the owners there very quickly and became close to Robert and his family who were all part of the business. They had a well-designed menu offering mediterranean and creole-inspired dishes. From the main dining room, you would go through a doorway into their jazz club. I love jazz, and so I started hanging in there. During the week, they would have local acts, but on weekends, they had international acts. When you went into the dining room, they had this ethereal decor that was soft and beautiful, and the music added to the ambiance.

The servers were beautiful and well-cast for this environment. Robert and Ben were great casting directors for their staff. I understood that because high-end salons like the ones I worked in do the same thing. On my first night there with a group of friends, we got seated right at the entrance to the dining room where we could see everybody. I was taking everything in and was happy and excited. The next thing I know, this tall, lean, model-looking guy with long dreads comes to the table to introduce himself as Calvin and let us know he was our waiter. I was mesmerized by him. He was so gorgeous.

One night after his shift, Calvin was changing from his all-black uniform, and he came out with white linen pants and shirt on.

And I thought, *Oh my god*. He asked if I wanted to hang out with him and his friends. We went down to the waterfront to a club and had a great time. A friendship developed between us and 90 percent of the time he was my waiter. Our friendship lasted a long time, even after he left Zanzibar and moved to New York and I moved to Atlanta. While there was always an attraction with us, it never went beyond friendship. I also had a crush on one of the waitresses, who looked like a prettier version of Tracy Chapman. We even went out one night and something she said made me uncomfortable about having had sex with a man when angry with an ex of hers. Was she saying that my dating both men and women didn't matter to her? What was she getting at? I was always like a detective digging for stuff even on a first date.

Soon, the people I met there, including Robert and his staff, began coming to me as clients, and I started hanging out with them. Tracy Chapman went there to eat one night. I was trying to get a date with her. I had all the girls on alert in case she came in. Turned out, she was with her manager, who was her partner.

So, I just loved everything about that club. I was there so much, people used to think I worked there or that I owned it. I was working in the Bellevue Hotel's Salon, which was like a Ritz Carlton, and I started sending our clients there. We always had local clients and guests who were staying at the hotel as well. On any given night, I would go in to the club and people thought I was a hostess because I knew and greeted so many people. Robert and the whole staff always gave me and my guests the white-glove treatment. I brought a friend there whose sister was in town from college, and I said to the chef, "She's a vegetarian." The chef in the back provided this whole array of vegetarian stuff on the house.

Sometimes, I would go there two or three times a week, including almost every Saturday. We would go to dinner and listen to jazz. I had no problem being in the back room by myself listening to jazz and the food was fabulous.

Robert used to send me some of the people that work there to get their hair cut. One of them, Wendy, was a waitress. She was very pretty, kind of Michelle-Pfeiffer looking. We became good friends. She even called me when Tracy Chapman came in. One day, while sitting in my chair, Wendy admitted that she was in love with Robert. While I was doing his employees' hair, they would all proclaim their love for Robert and their desire to marry him and have his children. This was getting funny. Were they telling me this because they thought I had some kind of relationship with him or just because women confide in their hairdressers?

Benjamin, Robert's brother, was cute and whimsical, but he was the opposite of Robert. I knew I could go to Benjamin for some things and Robert for others. I loved Ben like a brother, but I really had a big crush on Robert. They treated me beautifully. Robert and I had a great respect for each other's business sense, and he even offered to open up a salon for me. I went there one night on a date with this international lawyer, and we were in the jazz room. He was my client, but I thought, *I'll go out with him.* He wanted to set me up in my own salon in one of those countries like Saudia Arabia, maybe Kuwait, but I was not going anywhere near there. This guy only knew me from behind the chair which was very professional. He didn't know my temperament or my mouth. I still laugh to this day about it because they would've had my head the minute I got off the plane. Not for me! Benjamin comped the whole meal. I think he could feel my unease. I brought several of the people I dated to Zanzibar Blue and always knew that Robert or Ben had my back. I still look back on them and that time fondly. I really was in my element there and felt so seen and trusted for who I am. I've even written some poetry about that time.

One night, I went there on a date with a woman who was a friend of a friend. I wasn't really attracted to her at all. She was like nothing like my friends thought I would be interested in, and I wasn't. When she showed up dressed the way she was, it was a turnoff. My friends would say, "Elaine is not a racist. She's a Lookist. If you don't look good, you're out?" I dated intentionally for four years after Paul without hooking up with anyone. I went on so many dates with very nice people and had a great time. My therapist would ask, "Well, what's wrong with this one? They have a crooked nose or something?" God forbid they were late and forget no shows. One time I just left. I was just like that. And forget it if you happened to be Irish. Growing up we weren't even allowed to bring "Medigans" home! So those people never even got a kiss. My cousins, both men and women alike, were all handsome and stunning. So, I had very high standards.

On this date with this girl, I can't even remember her name, everybody was coming over to say hello to me. That was the way all the people were in there. We were sitting and looking at the menu and everybody's coming over to say hi. I was introducing her to owners, the manager, and the staff. They were the kind of people you saw magazines. My date was dressed like a butch lesbian construction worker. We were eating and drinking, and somebody came over to clean up right away or ask if we needed anything. We weren't having an intimate alone time, and she was very uncomfortable, so when we left, she stated, "I will never go there again!"

"What are you talking about? That's my favorite place and I go there all the time. They all know me," I said. She said, "I was waiting for them to come over and shine my shoes or something. They were all around doing everything for you." "Yeah, that's the idea of going to places like that where people know you and appreciate your loyalty," I wasn't interested in her and that was the end of that. They treated me like a princess and family, and I loved that.

Robert offered to open a salon for me, and I really appreciated it, but I never wanted those ties with anyone. I had several offers of people wanting to open a salon for me, including my father, which I would never do. I didn't want any financial or business ties with him. Robert was a great guy, and a great businessman. That was one of the things I loved about him. He just had class and charisma. They all had class, all his people. I realize now that I really didn't want to be tied down. I liked the freedom to travel and take on new challenges.

Dad Gets Out and Screws Up Again

So, my dad gets out of jail. And I wasn't talking to him for years at that point. I said to my therapist, "Diane, you know, he's getting out." And Bunny was laying her guilt trip on me. "Oh, if you don't talk to him, if something happens, you're going to feel so bad." And of course, my grandmother was begging me to talk to him. Finally, I gave in. I told my therapist, "I guarantee you, within a year, he will be back in jail." I was wrong, he made a liar out of me… it was 14 months.

While my dad was out of jail, I was downplaying dating women because I knew he had beaten up my cousin for being in a lesbian relationship. Also, I planned a combined birthday and industry party for myself that I wanted to take place at Zanzibar Blue. My list kept growing as usual to over 125 people. The room we wanted to use was over the jazz and dining room, and we would've created too much noise.

I decided to do a big 38th birthday party because I didn't want people to know when my 40th birthday happened. Unbeknownst to me, I would be leaving the city by the time I was 40. We had the party in the old Camac Bathhouse that had been abandoned and was now a gay center. I had a wonderful team of architects, designers, and friends who helped me decorate to resemble a bathhouse. I hired my favorite band from Zanzibar and a DJ. The invitations said, "black and white, leather and lace." It caused an uproar in my family because most didn't make the invite list. Only my mom, my Aunt Marian, a few cousins, my sister, and nephew were invited. The rest of the guest list were a diverse group of friends from the salon, Zanzibar, the industry, and my life.

And then there was my dad. Recently out of prison, he brought homemade red wine from South Philly. I asked him not to bring too much which I regretted, because it was gone in an instant. The food was all Italian, some of which I had prepared, including the gravy. I guess the wine worked on me because I lost all fear of my dad and was dancing with men and women of all ethnicities. My father said it was like the Italian coming out party—as big as a wedding. The only other thing he said to me was I should've had someone from South Philly do the catering.

I had already taken my father to Zanzibar, so he was a little prepared because he met some of my friends there. He loved the food there and all the special treatment he got being with me. They didn't even have cell phones back then, but my dad had some kind of walkie talkie in his hand while he was walking around the place. But Robert knew a lot about my dad, because I would talk to him about it.

Dad was out for 14 months, and of course, he got caught delivering cocaine to somebody right around the corner from his house. He always thought that he could defy the law. Duh! They followed him every time he was out on probation. It was very optimistic of him and in blatant defiance of the cops. He hated the cops. I also believe that's why he never ratted anyone out. He would not give the cops that kind of satisfaction. Ratting on anyone wasn't in his demeanor, and he knew the stakes. We all did. I mean, he really believed he could do whatever he wanted. You have to give him credit for that one.

So, then he goes back to jail and here's where it got really bad. They had just implemented in Pennsylvania that law, "three strikes, you're out," and if convicted, you must serve your new sentence plus any early release time from prior crimes. There were times they had let him out on good behavior without serving all his time. So, with his third strike, they added all that early release time to the new drug trafficking charges. This meant that he basically got life, roughly 40 years.

I then met Lynn who was from LA and was attending Vanderbilt in Nashville for her MBA, and we started dating. I introduced her to my family, and some were caught off guard because she was Chinese. My father did get to meet her when he was out of jail and we were at my grandmother's house, which was a very safe place for that initial meeting. His response to me was, "I always knew you were a lesbian." So now I was free. I started hanging a little bit more with lesbians, because up until that point, I was still dating both guys and girls.

As Lynn and I started dating more seriously, we began going back and forth from Philly to Nashville, Nashville to Philly. I wasn't going to Zanzibar as much as I used to. I brought a bunch of women in, a bunch of my lesbian friends. I saw Robert in the back, and I said to my server, "Tell Robert I want to say hi to him." And they came back to say, "Robert's really busy tonight." He began giving me the cold shoulder. He still came to me for his hair styling at the Bellevue Salon, so we saw each other but when I would go there, it wasn't the same after that. I could feel it was different. I really loved Robert, but knew it could never work for many reasons.

When I moved away, that really sealed the deal. When I told him I was going to move, I said, "I'm still going to send you clients. I meet people from all over," and I did. No matter where I was, when I met people and found out they were from Philly, I'd send them to Zanzibar. "When you're in Philly, go to Zanzibar Blue." It was such a fabulous time of my life. Everything seemed to come together, and I was able to date who I wanted. After being with Paul all those years of abuse and drama, I could feel my heart opening back up. I could remember sitting in the backroom of the salon, talking with my buddies. We all used to go over there after work, and I remember thinking I really loved Robert. Being able to really feel that love and take it in was fabulous.

But after moving away and traveling a lot, I just drifted away. They eventually opened other restaurants in the area. They have a whole corporation now and are still very successful, and I visit their other restaurants when I'm in Philly.

Once, I got in a fight with one of my friends who I don't talk to anymore. We were arguing about something, and she said, "I don't want to hear anything anymore about that Zanzibar Blue and how they treated you like a queen. Blah, blah, blah." I said, "You don't understand. It was one of the best parts of my life." People talk about the best parts of their life, and it all goes back to the love thing. Food is love; music is love. People you meet who become family, who treat you with love have a tremendous effect on you. They get your attention, and they give you attention, and it's love. There are certain restaurants that give you that feeling. You become part of the family in a restaurant like that.

Combining the love for food that feeds the soul, love in its own way, and the way that they treated me all made this a very special place at that time in my life. It was a center of fun for me, and I was looking for love in different places. Connecting to that love was food, music, caring, conversation, and attention. It was what I craved, and I found it there with those people at a time when I really needed all of that in my life. I feel like my time at Zanzibar Blue was a real coming of age, a time when I began to truly grow up and define who I was and who I wanted to be.

Lynn and Synagogue

Lynn (Ev) and I were together for six years. How we met is an interesting story. The night we met, I was all dressed up to go to Zanzibar Blue before and after a gathering at the synagogue celebrating Pat and Sharon's 9th anniversary. This is called an Oneg Shabbat. I had these brand-new shoes on that I loved, pastel pink, pointy heels, you know the drill. "I'll be back later tonight," I told my Zanzibar friends. The synagogue was right in the middle of Center City. I certainly wasn't expecting to meet anybody there. I went to sit down in the pew near my friend Jay. Next to him was an Asian woman and so I wound up sitting next to Ev. I thought she was pretty cool looking. Her style was kind of Gap, preppy looking, totally different from me. I sat there tapping my toes because I was so happy with my pretty new shoes.

After the ceremony, they had food. Lynn and I we were the only two Gentiles there. We bonded talking about food, restaurants, and California. She told me that she was new in town and only there temporarily on an internship, so I said, "Have you been to this restaurant or this place?" naming some of my favorites. "No, but I'd like to go to those places," she said. She had always been a foodie. I told her, "Well, I'm going back to this place that I hang at—Zanzibar Blue. The food is great, and they have live jazz music. Why don't we see if Jay wants to go?" Jay agreed. He is gay and at some point, I asked him, "How come you never introduced her to me? I know you fixed her up with other people." "Look at the two of you," he said. "You are so opposite." He never set me up with any of his female friends. In truth, they all just looked and seemed too boring for me. I would have never dated any of those people, so I got it. "Look at the two of you. I would never put you two together," he said and laughed.

This is truly where the Mafia Princess lesbian comes in. I would dress in the latest fashion and hip, feminine attire. At the time that I came out, I was going to Al Anon and OA meetings a lot, and they had their own LGBT groups, but if I went into those rooms, nobody dressed like me. The meetings were only nine blocks from South Philly, where I grew up, but when I moved into Center City, I was hanging out with a whole different group of people, but I never let go of my South Philly ways. I was all about my makeup, my clothes, my shoes, my hair.

I even spent 18 months going to AA, even though I'm not an alcoholic. My therapist questioned me often about why I was going to those meetings. I finally realized that I didn't want to go to the OA room because the AA rooms were more fun with more interesting attendees who always complimented my outfits. Lots of gay boys! Lynn was not the makeup type, but she looked hot in her nice jeans with her LA vibe. She had short, dark hair and she never even wore fingernail polish. One time, after we started dating, we were going to my Christmas party, and I said, "Let me make you up." I put all this makeup on her, and she looked beautiful. I showed the pictures to her family because I thought she looked so great but could tell they thought she looked like a whore. It was a clash of cultures!

That first night, a little group of us went to Zanzibar. Of course, everybody began coming over to the table, all my friends that work there. I had a good time as always. I was still flirting with the guys. When we left and they were getting ready to drop me off at my apartment, I said to Ev, "Let's get together some time to go out to eat or something." "I'll call you, or you call me." I gave her my number. Apparently, after I got out of the car, Jay said to her, "She'll never call you. She's a bitch." His comment made her afraid of me. She was shocked when I called her, and she told me what he said. While I liked Jay, he could've just said that I was very picky. We started dating and I found out that she had to go back to Nashville at the end of the summer to finish her MBA at Vanderbilt.

I went to Paris soon after we met for education and fun. Paris was everything I expected and more. It was so exhilarating—the food, the wine, the people, and, of course, the classes. After I got back from Paris, I would get some days off in a row to go visit her at school. When she had breaks, she would drive straight through from Nashville to Philly. It's not a fun drive, but she was young, 11 years younger than me.

I loved visiting Nashville. I was repping an Italian color line, so I was teaching and doing some sales. There was a fabulous salon there who was part of our guild, and I went there to teach classes as well. I always had this dream of moving to New York. I thought, perfect, after school, Lynn can get a really good job in New York, and we could move there together. After she graduated, she got hired by Southern Pizza Hut in management. The options were Charleston, Nashville, or Charlotte. I asked all my clients what they thought was the best choice, and they all said, "Go to Charlotte. It's more advanced. I called my client who had moved to Charleston. She said, "Oh, no. The gay community in general are very uppity here." They were very close knit in Charleston.

Tenacity

One of the things I learned from Susie Q was tenacity. Because there were weeks and months that I was not allowed to go to my Agnes grandparents; she had to navigate how we could see each other. As I got older, I realized when she came to see me, Louis, and Sadie during the school week, she always took us to the Italian sandwich shop. *Was there anything else?* It was prearranged with her and my mom. My grandfather Lou knew nothing about it. I could see all the joy and happiness on her face. Most of the time, she walked from her house to our school which was close to two miles. My grandmother could have taken the bus, but knowing her, I'm sure she saved the bus fare to buy us lunch. I was always aware of her joys and pain. My grandmother always acted like she was dumb or stupid.

She would say, "I don't know; I'm just a dumb girl from Brooklyn!" What dumb? She was as shrewd as a fox. And from Brooklyn? Brooklyn and stupid don't go together. So, *cut the crap Susie Q.* A year or two before she died, she finally started talking about her will. "I want to leave you and Tony the house, and Celeste. But I want to make sure your father always has a place to live." I said,

"You know, Grandma, he already has a big, beautiful house around the corner that he hardly uses." I did not add that he was always in jail. I did say, "If you leave this house to him or me and Toni, he is going to torture us. It's about him until we give it to him. I don't want any part of this. Leave it to Toni." I just knew somehow; he would scam us, and I was done with him. So, as soon as my grandmother died, we had the will read to us. Miss "Dumb" Grandmother had it all rigged up and with the lawyer that the house was left to five of us, but while he was alive, we were to take care of it and rent it out. And the worst of it was that we were to send him the rent money to prison for his commissary. And he still had his house and cars around the corner.

I was out. No way did I want to be a part of this is. All I saw was trouble ahead. Very true. He went crying to my Aunt Rita and my cousin Toni saying that I wouldn't help him, and they were going to get the house anyway. I was so happy that they decided to take care of it. One day, my cousin Toni called me to tell me that he had an antique car dropped off at her house and that my father wanted her to talk to the guy who brought it to see what it needed and for her to take care of it. I just laughed and didn't say what I wanted to say. So instead, I said, "He's all yours." Then Toni asked me, "Why does he want a French cookbook sent to him in prison? What cookbooks?" He also wanted her to send him the Bon Appetit magazine. "Don't you know what he does in prison?" I asked. She knew nothing about this.

He cooked for the fucking guards and a few other people. Then, I told her the story of what my grandmother would do while we were sleeping upstairs, meaning my grandfather in his bedroom without her and me in my room. One morning, I think it was maybe 5:00 a.m., I heard her downstairs tinkering around in the kitchen and then heard a man's voice. I went downstairs to see what was going on, and there was my grandmother handing off big trays of lasagna and gravy and meatballs to my father's prison guards. I couldn't believe it. She did it all before my grandfather got up.

I was maybe in my twenties at that time. Unbelievable. Toni was amazed.

I don't know if anyone knew this or not, but I think my grandfather was very tight with money, and she was very careful about how much she cooked every night. But Judge Higginbottom was right in the article where he said my father, Louis Agnes, would prostitute his own mother if he could. That article was a source of shame and embarrassment for me for many years. That article was on the internet and the one stating that my father was an associate of Angelo Bruno. Toni then understood about the cookbooks. He would have some of his friends, the guards or whoever pick up the ingredients for him, and then when the commissary was all cleared out, he would cook for his buddies, the guards.

My father, Louis Agnes Sr., was just unbelievable, way too much for me to deal with. It's not like Toni and my sister didn't know what he was like, but he promised them both at different times that he was leaving them everything. I knew better. My cousin and my Aunt Rita had to pay thousands in back taxes because he didn't pay the tax bills. They were done. He went crying to my sister Sadie that Toni screwed him over. That was always his thing. And he told my sister that he was going to leave the house to her son, his only grandson. Once again, bullshit.

And he caused another problem between Sadie and the tenant renting my grandmother's house. The tenant was bringing the rent to my sister Sadie, and she was supposed to send some to my dad and the rest was to go to taxes. Sadie was also paying rent to my dad for living in his house. My father didn't want to pay the taxes. He wanted all the money to go to him in jail. My father called the tenant and told her that she needed to send him the rent money directly to jail. My sister was unaware of this arrangement and sent the tenant a notice to pay back rent or be subject to eviction. The tenant went over to the house and beat the crap out of my sister. Eventually, my father sent a friend to threaten the tenant, who got scared and left. He also sent someone who was supposed to be a cop to threaten Sadie because he had someone lined up who was going to fix it up to earn more rent. None of them ever listened to me.

So, my sister was forced to find a place to live with my nephew and their dog. My heart was breaking for them, but that's what happens when you engage with him. You might ask why he needed so much money in prison. He had special privileges to make calls all the time, and he wanted money for his upgrades in prison or to pay off people. Everyone gets hurt dealing with the devil and that devil was Louis Agnes, Sr.

Oh Dear! Yankees in Georgia

When I started my relationship with Ev, we were going back and forth to California to visit her family, vacation, or to spend holidays there. Our time there was also spent exploring so many other areas near and far. To this day, the Big Sur is at the top of the list of favorites. The Pacific Ocean is magnificent and so are the views when you're driving up or down Highway 1.

I thought when we decided to move to Charlotte that we were only moving there for her internship, and in my mind, I believed we were going to go live in California. I wanted to live in Santa Monica. And even though I interviewed at some fabulous salons, it never worked out. We did look for places there, but I asked her this question recently. "Did you really ever want to go back to LA or were you just stringing me along?" She said, "If I had gotten a really good job there, I would have gone back." She travels all the time anyway, but she didn't want to live in New York. She hates the cold.

I had to make a decision at that point. I was still flying back and forth to Philly. I wasn't ready to give years of wonderful established customers, friends, and family and all my business relationships that I worked very hard to maintain. I was flying back and forth to Philly from wherever I was and spending ten days every four or five weeks. So, finally, I said, "Look, I can't stay in Charlotte. There's no way I'm staying here." "They offered me the Myrtle Beach area," she said. "There is no way on heaven or on earth that I'm ever moving there," I replied. "So, this is what we're going to do. You either have to find somewhere that I'm willing to live or I'm leaving, and we can work that out later on down the line."

She went to Atlanta for business, and when she came back home to Charlotte, she said, "I think I found a place for you that you would like, that we would both like to live." We went to Atlanta for my birthday in February. People were walking around wearing shorts and jogging. She took me to areas with big restaurants and everybody was outside. It was great. Most of all, there were about five very famous salons that were on the Intercoiffure list of Top Salons around the world. That really did it.

I liked the whole vibe. I've always known that the contacts you make along the way are very important. You've got to use your contacts. I have always known to stay connected. That's how I went from a hairdresser in South Philly to the top of my career. So, when I moved to Atlanta, and bear in mind, I never thought in a million years I would be working in Atlanta, I had contacts in place. When I was in New York, hanging out with my bosses, I was never afraid to go up to anyone and shake their hands. I don't have a problem with making connections. Again, I observed that from my family growing up. With my bosses, we would be wining and dining famous people from Europe and all over the world. I used my connections wisely. I met Jameson Shaw there, his brother, and his daughter. Other girls would shy away from being with all these men. Not me. I shook their hands. I stayed there for the conversations and observed. I asked them questions. I have taught classes on this, and I advise any young people or others who want to move up in any industry to learn this. Who would have known that I would have come to Atlanta and would want to work at the salons owned by these very famous people I had met along the way? When I was moving here, I went and interviewed, and they hired me on the spot. They already knew me.

Within a year, I had built my book. We made a poster saying I trained in Paris, and I put those all around the area. I offered a free glaze with every haircut. It's a color service, a glaze to gloss up your hair. I got an award for going from zero to $30,000 in one year, building my clientele. That's huge. But again, I used my connections and that was everything.

Lynn and I bought a big, beautiful house in a great neighborhood close to Emory. Our area had some diversity. All the neighbors were from different areas and a few from different parts of the world. We didn't even have to go out of our little area because there were so many get togethers amongst ourselves. Lynn and I were so different. She wanted to play softball and was really into sports. I would say, "Go, go." I had a lot of my own things I wanted to do.

She was the manager of eleven restaurants in the Atlanta area. It was very, very hard, and she was often stressed out. If you know the restaurant business, it's exhausting and hard and these were chain restaurants. It was difficult as we were both adjusting to new jobs, our new lifestyle, and being away from our families. She had guys that were sleeping in the restaurants at night because their wives threw them out for always being at work. There was a guy who was stealing from her by manipulating things when people would bring in coupons. I forget how it worked exactly. I think he would give them the discount, but he would keep the money, and then throw the coupons away. They always have some clever way of stealing.

I was still travelling from Atlanta every month to see family and friends and take care of my clients. When in Philly, I would stay with my grandmother or with Pat and Sharon. After my grandmother Sue passed, I would always stay with Pat and Sharon. At that point, they had become family to me. Their extended Italian and Jewish families were like my own.

When they decided to have children and Pat got pregnant, I was totally stoked. Since I was staying there 10 days of every month, I was able to watch the baby grow. I happened to be there the day Daniel was born and I never knew my heart could burst so big. I didn't feel like Danny was getting enough to eat, and I was worried that he was going to die so I made a big stink just like my grandfather had done with me. We still laugh about it to this day. I fell instantly in love with Danny and then Sophie. I never knew our friendship would last 40+ years. I also didn't know that both their children would become like my own children. I am their aunt and godmother.

Meeting Pat and Sharon was one of the best parts of my adult life. They were with me through a lot of my growth. Meeting them and their families, getting to know and be a part of their families was a wonderful change for me. My family life shifted, and I had to become stronger, more independent, and adjust to losing the people who were dearest to me. Pat and Sharon were there to guide me and be by my side. Losing my grandmother Sue early on was traumatic. I talked to my grandmother Sue every day, sometimes multiple times.

Once she was gone, I still kept thinking about calling her all the time. I realized instead that I needed to call my friends or my aunts and cousins. Having Pat and Sharon there meant and still does mean the world to me. Also, having friends and meeting people from the 12-step rooms means all the difference between feeling crazy and feeling sane. Not that we all don't have our crazies but learning and working the saying "talk to each other and reason things out and let there be no gossip or criticism" has been a lot for me to practice and learn. I've learned how to behave in a manner that just wasn't modeled for me. I have always said Al-Anon saved my life and Ma made it worth living.

Not having children has been a big loss in my life. And even though I never gave birth to children, that might be a good thing. My therapist has told me that I might've ended up in jail protecting them. I have adored and been blessed by certain young people in my life. Having my godchildren, Danny and Sophie, and my nieces and nephews and watching them grow up by my side means the world to me. All of them are a big part of my life and world.

Never Trust the Quiet Ones

Lynn and I ended up in an ugly breakup. She cheated on me, and it was the weirdest thing. I am so sensitive and weirdly intuitive. One of her employees was some sort of low-class southern girl, Tammie Sue. She looked like somebody that grew up on a farm. Her haircut was disastrous to me, and her clothes weren't any better. I knew something was off. We would go to this gay and lesbian church that we liked, that had just moved into our neighborhood, and one day Lynn said, "Let's go to this other church because my friend who works for me wants us to go out after church for something to eat and to meet her partner. We went out to breakfast, and I asked the girl, "How did you two meet?" I felt her kick Lynn under the table. She answered, "We were out to lunch with her and her ex-partner, and we were flirting under the table. After that, we hooked up and that was it." This is what she was telling me about her and her girlfriend. So, I got up and excused myself because I felt ill. I knew that if one more word was spoken, I was going to throw her over the table. "You know what? I need a breath of fresh air right now," I said, and I went to the bookstore next door. After they left, Lynn and I got in a big fight.

Another time, Lynn was going white water rafting and taking her employees. We were sitting at the breakfast table and Tammie Sue showed up. "Oh, she's going to drive with me to the place where we start the rafting and then she'll drop me off home," Lynn said. But the minute Tammie Sue walked through the door, my stomach sank, and I felt like I would throw up. I thought, *I haven't had a feeling like this in a long while.*

Something was telling me she was cheating. I had felt it even before that morning because her habits had changed. I'm like a detective. I don't need you to tell me anything. I feel your habits. One night, Lynn called me and said they had to get one of the restaurants cleaned up and do all the floors before the morning because they were getting inspected. "You have employees, but you're staying there to mop the floors?" I asked. "Where are you going to sleep?" "I'm going to get a hotel somewhere nearby," was her answer. I knew she was lying. She was the fucking manager of eleven stores, and she was hanging out to mop? She never once mopped at home.

One day, I got a call from her while I was at work at the Ritz in Atlanta. "What time are you coming home today?" she asked. "I'm not done until six o'clock," I answered. "So, you're not going to be at the house at all?" she asked. I knew exactly what she was doing. She was going to the house with Tammie Sue. I ran out of the salon like a mad woman, got in my car, and I drove home. I don't know what she did or if she changed her mind but somehow, she must have known I was on to her. I had this plan that if they were there, I was going to throw this bitch outside with no clothes on and fucking soak them with the hose. That's what I had in mind. But by the time I got home, nobody was there. I went back to work. I was very crazy.

Then it was our anniversary, and we took our friend Jay out for his birthday. We came home and we were going to the pool. We had our whole day planned. "I just gotta go upstairs to my office and check a few things first," Lynn said. I started to head to the pool ahead of her, but I forgot something. I had opened the door and closed it again, so she thought I left, but I had never gone out. I overheard her say, "Oh yeah, she wants to go to the pool. I have to go meet her and we'll swim, and then we're coming home to have a romantic dinner. Then she's going to want to make love." And then there was silence, and Tammie Sue must have said something like, "Well, when are you going to tell her?" I could figure it all out. And then I heard Lynn say, "I don't want to do it on our anniversary."

I was in shock and my throat and mouth felt like it was slowly filling up with cotton. I couldn't talk. She heard me and came down the steps. She realized I heard everything. "What were you doing listening to my conversation?" she said. "Don't you dare turn this on me," I yelled back at her. "You gotta be kidding. You gotta be fucking kidding." At that point, a furious argument ensued, and I really wanted to hurt her.

I went into our bedroom and called my sponsor. "I'm gonna fucking kill her," I said. "Get to a meeting as quick as possible," was my sponsor's answer. So, that's what I did, and it made a big difference to talk to my people. The next day, I called my therapist, and she said, "See if she will come in with you." She did.

This went on for a few weeks, and after a few meetings, the therapist said, "The best thing I think you two should do is sleep together." Lynn had cut things off with Tammie Sue, so I thought. I had thrown Lynn out of the bedroom. So, I allowed her back into our room and one night, she was lying in bed and said, "I have to finish one thing and I'll be down." She figured I'd fall asleep. I was looking at the clock and I tiptoed to the bottom of the steps. I heard her telling Tammie Sue everything the therapist told us to do. I went ballistic and I ran up those steps screaming like a maniac. She was still on the phone, and I said, "You better get off that fucking phone, because I'm gonna rip it out of your hand." First, this girl was her employee. Lynn wasn't out at work. Lynn's big manager liked me, and I told her that I was going to call him and out her and this affair with a staff member. She began crying, sobbing. "Please don't call him. Please don't call him." "I'm fucking calling him," I said. "I have his home number." She was hysterical, sobbing, begging me. I stopped and I said, "Let me tell you something. I'm done. We're breaking up." I was livid. All the rage and disappointments over people abandoning me flooded my senses. I started throwing her computer around and tossing everything off her desk. She dropped the phone and began screaming, but she wouldn't touch me. She's not that type of person. "Don't you know who you're dealing with?" I screamed at her. I knew I needed to get out of the room before I did something I would regret later.

I went to the therapist on my own that week. "I'm afraid I'm going to hurt her because one day she was peeling something at the kitchen sink, and there was a knife in the sink. I thought, *I could take this knife and fucking slice her throat open.* And then another morning, I was leaving for work, pulling out of the driveway, and she was at the mailbox, and I thought, *I can take this car and make it act like it swerved, and hit the mailbox and the wooden part will just smash her down and kill her.* I've never hurt anybody." My therapist said, "Both of you need to get in here." And she told Lynn, "You need to move out for your own safety."

Lynn is very tight with her family. The Asian people have a particular way they do things. To get that house that we wanted when we first moved to Atlanta, we didn't have enough money. We were looking at houses all over the area but didn't find anything we liked. Finally, our realtor took us over to a house that his cousin hadn't even put on the market yet and we absolutely loved it. We needed to borrow some money for the downpayment, but Lynn's parents didn't want to give **us** any extra money. They only wanted to give **her** extra money.

I said, "I'm not doing this unless the title goes on both our names. She didn't think they would lend us the money unless the house was in her name without me. "You know what?" I said. "I'd rather go find a smaller place. I trade services with architects, builders, all kinds of contractors, and if you think I'm going to use all my trade money I'd be making for this house that you think is going to be all yours? Think again. Talk to them." "I can't talk to them because my Chinese isn't that good, and they don't speak English," she said.

"Let me talk to them," I said. "Get your sister on the phone. She speaks English and Chinese." And that's what she did. I am the type of person that you can't bullshit. Believe you me, my name was on that deed when we bought the house. I wasn't playing and thank God I did that. When we broke up and finally sold the house, I got my half of the profits to be able to move on and buy my own place and two others.

We stayed in the house while putting it on the market. She moved into another bedroom. We found a realtor and my friend Lee, who is an architect and designer, came for the weekend to fix the patio for showings. We figured it would be helpful for the sale if he could make it look beautiful. That was his joy in life. Lee was outside working, and the realtor guy left. We were getting ready to sign the listing for the house.

I realized it was over and our beautiful house and our lives together were done. Something snapped in me, and I started throwing chairs around the house, throwing them at her. She ran up to the top of the steps, put her hand on her hip, and said, "I cheated on you, so what?" "Get OUT!" I screamed. I was a maniac. Lee was outside. I ran up those steps after her. She is a tall person, and she isn't tiny. I screamed the loudest scream I've ever screamed in my whole life. In my head I was just tapping her, but I threw her up against the wall in the bedroom. She fell into the corner. She was hysterical because she knew I was crazy at this point. She probably knew she might have lost her life that day if she did something else. And I just screamed at the top of my lungs, "Get the fuck out of this house as fast as you can."

Lee, of course, thank God, came running in. "What's going on?" he said. "Lynn, I think you need to leave." So now she was sobbing and began getting a suitcase together. She called her trashy friend to come and pick her up. "You better not let her come up the street," I said. "You better get in your own car, and you better go." So that's what happened. And the best part about the story is that later that night I put on a really hot purple bob wig, and Lee and I went to the gay men's club. I was dancing up a storm, having a blast like nothing had happened. I was done with her ass and her lying. After getting through the gritty part of my life, nothing was going to take me down.

Nobody wants to be cheated on. And I think the bigger thing is, no one wants to be lied to. If you don't want to be with me, say you don't want to be with me. Have the guts to say, "Look, I don't want to be with you anymore. I've met someone else that I really want to be with and before I make a mess of things and start a relationship with this person, I want to be honest. I have feelings for them. It's going somewhere. I don't want to be with you anymore." Hearing something like that is terrible, but you can live with that, right? It's hard when people can't be honest. There's nothing you're going to do or say to them to make them tell the truth.

If you lie to me, I'm going to lose it. It's the lying that makes me truly go nuts. And I think that's the real problem here. I grew up with a lot of lies and deceit. It takes me back to my childhood of never knowing the truth, never knowing who's telling me the truth, and being, in a sense, cheated on by my father. He cheated on me and my siblings with his other kids from the other families he created. He was more attentive to other people, treated the other kids like they mattered, and my siblings and I didn't; like we weren't important enough to bother with. That's a terrible feeling. When Lynn cheated, I was filled with rage.

Lynn and I had a great life together. We had investments and we went away all the time. We both loved to travel. That was our best thing. She was a great partner who came home all the time. We made terrific meals together and had lots of fun dinner parties. She was that kind of partner, and I was, too. We were great at traveling together. I can't tell you how much we traveled, like every quarter, when she had time off, we went somewhere new. I don't know why she wanted to destroy all that, but she did, and I moved on.

Lynn called me a year later. It was when I had my breasts done, and I was laying there recovering. "What do you want?" I asked. She was crying, sobbing her eyes out. "She cheated on me," she said. "Oh, what a shame," I laughed. "I need somebody to talk to every morning. I'm alone." "Really?" I answered. "And you think that person's going to be me?" I asked. "You are insane." Then the next question, honest to God, the next question was, "Well, do you know anybody that you can hook me up with or go out with?" I think she wanted me to say, "I'll take you back." Yeah. That was not happening. I said, "Are you fucking for real? You want me to hook you up with somebody? You're fucking crazy."

When we moved out, I had a nice art collection. Not Picassos, but pieces she wanted to take including her birthday gift that wasn't done yet. I had contracted an artist to make it by trading services with her. "If you think I'm going to let you take any of this art to some fucking white trash tramp's house, or wherever you're going to live, not gonna happen. You're not getting the art. If you ask me again, I'm going to crack this fucking art over your head." After we had broken up, Lynn came up to me at a lesbian gathering and asked about the picture she never got for her birthday. "You're crazy," I said. "Don't ever ask me about that, especially in front of this lesbian group like I'm holding onto something that belongs to you."

Lynn would call would whenever she broke up with someone. "Please cut my hair," she would beg me. "No," I answered, but she showed up at the salon. The other workers said they could feel her regret. "She regrets breaking up with you," they told me. We have since tried to be reasonable with one another. Time makes it easier to forgive, maybe not forget, but to let go of some of the anger. One Christmas, she called me about the seven fishes meal we Italians do on Christmas Eve. I make calamari stuffed with ricotta and shrimp. "Are you making your calamari?" she asked. "If you're helping, I'll make it," I answered. She came for the meal and brought her newest girlfriend, a scientist of some sort. I could feel a sense of discomfort from her, so we didn't try that again.

I bought a smaller house near where I live now. It was about half the size of the house we lived in, but it felt like me. I put my art in it. I just had to move along. I admit that the thing that I loved about my relationship with Lynn was that she had family, even though they were in California. I liked being with someone who had family because when I left Philly, it was hard to leave my own family. My aunts were like, "Where are you going? How can you leave?"

My mom's oldest sister, my aunt Connie, asked, "Why are you leaving? And I said, "I'm going to go to California. We're going to move to California because we love it there and to be near Lynn's family." Aunt Connie and my Uncle Fred did not want their daughter Sheila to move abroad after medical school. She wanted to travel the world and go help people, something like Doctors Without Borders. Sheila came back because she didn't like the food and missed her mother's cooking. So, they bought her a humongous house with a carriage house, and they actually paid for her kids to go to school and everything. In my family, nobody left. I mean, you just did not leave.

My sister had no qualms about leaving at eighteen and went to San Francisco, then Florida, and eventually Italy for many years. She managed to escape and live her own life while I still enjoyed being around my family and felt obligated to my grandparents and mother. I was devastated when Lynn and I broke up, because here I was in Atlanta, alone with no family. I had made plenty of friends, but it was still upsetting to be so on my own because I had only been here three years.

My Big Skinny Greek Family

Eventually, I started going out more and I met a woman named Callie. She pursued me, and I had known about her through some of my other friends. She was gorgeous, very hot, and accomplished.

On top of all that, she was a multi-millionaire, having made her fortune in real estate. All of her siblings came to our salon, even her mom. I had seen her there, but I wasn't ready to date anyone seriously. It was only maybe eight or ten months after Lynn and I broke up, and I usually like to give myself a few years between relationships. But she had family, a big Greek family, which I found appealing. Greeks, Calabrians, and Sicilians are a lot alike. In a way, it was great, but in another way, the ruination of the relationship. Their dynamics were dysfunctional in a way I recognized.

On our first date, we went to this excellent restaurant, and it was with her family. So, when we got in therapy, the therapist said, "Well, what were you expecting when on the first date you're going out to eat with her family?" Yes, that should have been it, right? But for what it's worth, in my heart, I had this deep-seated feeling of, *if I meet someone, I want them to have a nice family.* Family was everything to me, you know. Along comes this person who has her mom, two sisters, and a big family who dominated everything. For example, when Callie was getting rid of her computers, she was going to give me one. I didn't have a computer at that time. They were at her house in two minutes to get all her stuff. Then she talked about giving me the Mercedes. I drove a very basic car, a Honda or something. "You should be driving a Jaguar," Callie said. "Well, if you want me to drive a Jaguar, get me one," was my answer.

Everything you hear about the Greek families is true. I must say I learned a lot from Callie and from the relationship. She encouraged me to do new things that I had always wanted to do like invest in real estate. We also went to a couples' workshop on how to get the love you want and need, and I learned how to navigate relationships better. Obviously, it didn't work with her. It couldn't work because in between sessions, the minute we went on break, she was on the phone with her real estate. I had always wanted to be someone like her—beautiful, smart, and a millionaire. After that, I changed my tune. I was already beautiful inside and out, and smarter than I ever knew. I'm still very grateful for that time with her and her family.

I decided that I was going to buy rental properties and either rent them out or flip them. It was a very fulfilling to utilize a broader range of my skills. And with her encouragement, I began buying other properties even after our relationship ended. Callie and I lingered for a total of about eighteen months. I knew the relationship was too restrictive for me when I wasn't allowed to eat desserts or carbs, and it needed to end. I tried to stay friends with her and her family, but it was too complicated.

Nonni and Nonno (great grandparents) in their home with a candelieri 1954

Uncle Bobby's wedding (clockwise from) little Elaine, Dad Louis, Mom Margie, Aunt Rita, Uncle Bobby, my godfather 1958

Aunt Marion's wedding (clockwise from the left) Comare Helen, Aunt Marion (the bride), Grandfather Lou, Comare Cassie, Cousin Linda, Elaine 1958

In Atlantic City with (left to right) Cousin Sandy, Aunt Celie, Mom, Elaine 1957

Elaine and Cousin Russell 1960

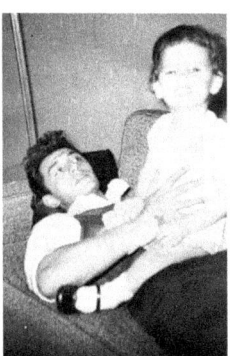

Uncle Bobby and Elaine 1956

Young Uncle Joe, Grandmother Stella, Mom 1952

Uncle Fred and Aunt Connie 1950

Four generations of Luigi Mallace: (left to right) Uncle Joe, Grandfather Lou, Great great Uncle Luigi from Italy, Little Louis, Great Uncle Joe 1980

Mallace siblings: (left to right) Aunt Teresa, Grandfather Louis, Aunt Louisa, Aunt Celie, Uncle Joe, Aunt Mary 1980

Cousin Sammy and his dog (center), Elaine, Debbie, Joann (clockwise) 1971

Aunt Marion, Elaine, Mom at
Elaine's 38th birthday party 1992

Cousins Sammy and Michael 1990

Mom and Uncle Dominic 1986

Mom, Nephew Julian, Sister Sadie,
Brother Louis, Elaine, Cousin Celeste
(clockwise from Mom in center) 1991

Dad in prison, visited by his mom,
my Grandmother Sue 1980s

*Pat and Elaine at Claudio's
Italian market in South Philly
shopping for cheeses 2008*

*Ma Jaya Sati Bhagavati teaching four
months before her passing 2012*

Sharon and Pat: my besties 2018

Pat, Sophie, Sharon and Danny 2018

Elaine in red fox hat, early 1990s

Younger Nina looking like k.d. lang 1991

Elaine heading to Red Carpet party in Atlanta 2008

Nina and Elaine at their wedding 2016

Mikey, Nina and Johnny on a Friday night having my homemade crabs and spaghetti! 2015

Elaine and Nina's first Christmas 2014

Elaine and Nina at home 2019

Elaine and Nina dressed up for brunch 2015

PART 3:

Eat, Pray, Love
New York Style

From MAFIA PRINCESS *to* LESBIAN CHIC

CHAPTER 13

THE BEST GURU IS THE ONE THAT MAKES YOU LAUGH

After I broke up with Callie, I knew I needed a new sponsor. I was having a hard time staying clean with my food. I found a new sponsor in OA who said that I really wasn't following my 12-step program. She was a well-regarded sponsor, and it was hard to get on her schedule. She finally had an opening, and we met. She had heard my story in the rooms and knew my background. She said, "You really haven't surrendered to your higher power. You really have not fully done your second and third steps." She recommended that I revisit my second and third steps and do them over.

Even though I didn't want to admit it, she was right, even though I had been in the program for years. In the program, you do your initial 12-step work, and then you continue doing step work every day and follow what you've learned. *Well, I've been to synagogues and many of the teachings there resonated with me. I've been to many churches and to many different places, and I honor all the things I've learned.* So, I started searching for, *what's my Higher Power?* And for the willingness to turn my will over to the care and power of that Higher Power.

A good friend of mine recommended I go to a class at Kashi At-lanta Ashram where she was teaching Sanskrit. They say when you have three people tell you something within a month, it's meant for you. That's a saying. Two other people came into the salon recom-mended Kashi to me. It was the same place my friend had said she was teaching Sanskrit. Kashi offered yoga, meditation, and spiritu-al growth. I took the signs to heart and went to Kashi Atlanta, and it changed my life forever.

Yoga in Atlanta - 1998

Many years prior, I had started to explore yoga, meditation, and Eastern philosophies and traditions. It had a profound impact on me, and yet, it scared the hell out of me. While I was used to doing aerobics and jogging, I never knew I had the propensity to get as high in meditation as I did. I found this peaceful tranquil place inside of me, but it scared me. At the time, I wasn't ready for this level of depth.

Kashi Atlanta was only in existence about a year or so before I found it. I was looking for a diverse form of spirituality, and there it was for me. There were altars to the Hindu goddesses and to the Mother Mary and Jesus, and this all felt great to me. Being familiar with Hinduism and their teachings from early on felt very com-fortable. I had never really gone the full length of my studies from the yoga center in Philly, and so when I landed at Kashi, I found an oasis in the center of Atlanta. Even though Atlanta had so many churches, it felt to me like a city without a soul.

Kashi became everything to me. Jaya Devi, the leader here in Atlanta, was on her way to becoming a Swami. I loved her yoga classes, which were highly spiritual, and I felt things there that I had never felt before. There were times I cried in yoga class as I was opening more and more. There are asanas in yoga that are heart opening. There is a way when you are in community with like-minded people who are also searching for the depth in their heart and souls that the alchemy is amazing. Jaya Devi was a tall, white, Irish girl from Boston and Tennessee. She reminded me of my Girl Scout leader that threw me out because I was complaining about walking home from the Lakes. When she said, "Well, I'm walking, too," I said, "Yes, but you are six feet tall with very long legs." I guess South Philly girls should not be Girl Scouts.

Jaya Devi is an amazing Yogi and brilliant at what she does. She had studied with many masters before she met Ma. She is wildly beautiful and probably the best yoga teacher I have had and learned from, of course, except for Ma. Jaya Devi had a very soft way about her, yet her strength was powerful. There were times I struggled with her and some of her ways. Also, as I've said, most of my teachers along the way were very strong Italian and Jewish women. I seem to vibe with them the best.

There was a bit of a culture clash for me in Atlanta to begin with. It doesn't have a strong Italian community like Philly or New York. Most of my friends here are Jewish, and of course Ma the Guru was just that, a very strong, Jewish woman from New York married originally to an Italian man. Jaya Devi was very sweet and cracked my heart open to the teachings of love and compassion. She prepared me to meet Ma. She once said to me, "You need to be around love as much as you can." I never clicked with the hierarchy of the ashram, so I struggled with this for years. I knew what I wanted and that was to get closer to Ma, and it wasn't happening in Atlanta. I always felt that I was being held back. We tried different approaches to bring us closer like our Hug Sadhana. Every time Swami and I saw each other, we hugged. None of it really worked out. I needed Italian hugs. I was belligerent as usual that we were told to stand when she walked into a room and fold our hands in Pranam. I was just as I was in the Girl Scouts when I got thrown out.

From the minute I got to Kashi Ashram, I loved it. I went all in for yoga and meditation. And people there who taught yoga were terrific. There were a few people that I already knew there, and one of my long-term friends, Lily, taught Sanskrit there and was a yogi and had travelled with many well-known Hindu teachers. The second week I attended there was a sign on the door that said Achariya Das was coming to teach meditation. I thought, *this sounds wonderful. I'm going to come to that.* And the friend that I started with didn't want to come. I thought, *I don't care if she comes or not; I'm going by myself.* And this is a big part of my story. Even though I have friends that I love to be with and hang out, I am never afraid to go places on my own. I do what I want, when I want, all by myself if I want. *This guy's a master. I have to go. This is what I need.* I was all excited.

I had been looking and waiting to find someone that I could learn from like the Indian Guru in Philly. I was going to meet this Indian Swami, and maybe he could help me deepen my relationship with God. This Swami walks in and I looked at him while we're chanting and I thought, *He doesn't look Indian. He looks Spanish, maybe Italian.* He was wearing an orange Punjabi and reminded me of the Catholic priests from my childhood. From the moment he started speaking, it was obvious to me that he was from New York. Turns out that he was Italian and very gay and mischievous. As he taught us meditation, he was very funny. I just was so amused. He talked about food the whole time during his meditation classes. He said things like, "I gotta use meditation. I'm thinking about that cheesecake waiting for me with the refreshments for after class." He had us all laughing. I've always liked people who could keep me laughing a lot. That's a big part for me.

Afterwards, we had a gathering with desserts and chai. I said to him, "You remind me of my ex." He said, "You remind me of my mother." We all laughed. This was all new to me. I didn't realize I was supposed to Pranam to him and show him reverence. I talked to him like he was in my family. At that time, he was coming to Atlanta to teach every few months. We hit it off, and I looked forward to seeing him every visit. One time when he came to visit, I made eggplant parmigiana, and he was immediately addicted. Food became a big thing between the two of us, both coming from big Italian families with the same traditions. It was kind of love at first sight, really. Some of the other Swamis would visit and teach and I got to know several of them. Kashi became my home for a very long time.

Meeting the Guru

Our ashram is dedicated to Neem Karoli Baba, a highly influential Indian saint and mystic. The core of his teachings is centered on love, devotion, and interconnectedness of all beings and attracted many Westerners. Ma Jaya Sati Bhagavati was an American-born, internationally renowned spiritual teacher, who was an activist, author, and artist. She founded the Kashi Ashram in 1976, following the teachings of Neem Karoli Baba and is also the mother of our yoga lineage, Kali Natha yoga. She won numerous interfaith awards in America and around the world. Ma gave love like crazy and was like the biggest Jewish mother.

When I started going to the Kashi Ashram here in Atlanta, I heard everyone talking about Ma this and Ma that. I was like, "Who is this Ma?" A lot of the gurus in India and spiritual people had the name "Ma." I could write another book just on how much my life changed by being part of this beautiful interfaith teaching at our ashram.

The first time I went to see her was when she came to Atlanta. Ma was coming to do a weekend intensive. Everyone at the ashram was buzzing. We were getting ready to host people from all over the world. I had never been to anything like this in my life. The place was packed like sardines. People were in their saris and the men in their Kurtas—a loose-fitting shirt worn with pajama-like pants. We started chanting and singing, and I fell in love with the music called Kirtan, a form of devotion. Our Kirtan at Kashi in Atlanta was fabulous and at that point it was all I knew.

I was seated towards the back, which was very unusual for me, but the front section of the floor was reserved for Swamis and her utmost devotees. Just the excitement, the singing brought me to a higher state, and I could feel my whole chest expanding. I had been practicing yoga for a while. We were encouraged to ask questions so, of course, my hand went up as soon as I could. I remember asking a question about my unworthiness, about my weight and eating disorder. All I remember was Ma's voice and my head and heart felt like an explosion going through me, something I had never felt before in my life. I never did acid, but it felt like something like that.

Just the excitement and singing brought me to a higher state. Her words and the vibration of her voice went right to my heart and soul. I could feel her love surge through me, and it made me want to cry. And every time after that when she spoke, it felt like that to me. Whether she was talking to me or others, it was magical, yes, but it was more than that. It was divine. I have been devoted to the ashram for more than twenty years and sat before her many times.

Kashi Ashram, the main one in Sebastion, Florida, sat on 68 acres. The first time I went there, there was a huge celebration for Ma's birthday with people from all over the world. My friend Linda drove us down. In my usual princess fashion, I had overpacked with new makeup, nice clothes, expensive shoes, and gourmet food for my host. Linda and I immediately got into a loud argument because she had me get out and wanted me to walk on this long, winding path to the manmade River in front of the house that Ma lived in. There were also other houses that the residents lived in with their families. When I saw the path, I screamed, "I am not walking on that dirt path! Do you realize that my brand-new shoes cost me $350?" She then hollered at me, "Please keep your voice down! There are people sleeping in the rooms right where you are standing! And there is a curfew here at 10 p.m. for loud talking so please use your inside voice." I giggled because she was always telling me that and my response would be, "What's an inside voice? This is my inside voice!" and "What are you doing with $350 shoes on at an Ashram?"

My dear Linda wanted me to walk down to the opening in front of the Ganga (Indian for River). In India, the rivers are very sacred as the ashes of their beloveds are buried there. The Temples were all lit up beautifully! And the beautiful fountain was spurting out water into the misty air. The irony of all that was that my Guru Ma was a fashionista and had lots of beautiful shoes and bags. Her birthday party was grand. There were so many people there to honor her, and there was also music from a few celebrities who were and are part of Kashi.

I loved the house and the person I was staying with. I did eventually make it down the path to see the Ganga the next night. There were also big tents and a music stage and fabulous festivities all weekend. I got to meet so many new people that were part of the ashram. I felt so welcomed and at peace on that first visit that I bought an investment property that I could use when visiting or to rent out.

One time, I remember thinking, *if there's anybody in the world I would love to spend an hour with it was Achariya Das.* I missed my scheduled flight home because I was shopping in downtown Melbourne, so I had to sit another four hours at the airport waiting for the next one. When I boarded the plane, I was so pissed and aggravated. Callie was supposed to pick me up, but she couldn't because I was coming in too late. I got on the plane, and I was sitting there, when all of a sudden, I felt somebody hit me on the back of my head. *What the fuck, who did this?* So, I turn around, I didn't see anybody. I thought, *oh, there's a kid back there, fucking hiding or playing.* I sat back in my seat because I couldn't see anybody and then I got another tap on the head. I looked back in anger, and there was Achariya Das crushed under the seat, giggling. There was nobody next to me, so he came and sat with me. *Oh my God, I thought, is this really happening?* "When are you going to come to New York and visit me?" he said. "I want you to come and visit." I was in love from the moment I saw him. So was everyone else!

We made a plan. I found time in my busy schedule to go there for a weekend. He picked me up in a van, and when I saw what was behind his seat, it made me laugh and you might think I was crazy it made me love him more. No, it was not a ring or a fur—IT WAS A BIG BASEBALL BAT! I cracked up because my Grandfather Tony and many other men in South Philly had them in the back of their car. I felt safe!

Ashram Italiano, When Dharma Meets Drama

When I got there, I was shocked at how big and beautiful the Ashram house was. I loved being in New York and Queens seemed so familiar to me. Forest Park was beautiful with its own downtown and great shops and restaurants. While out walking, I passed a street and had an overwhelming rush of feelings. I realized this was where my Aunt Connie and Uncle Fred lived when Russell and I were children. I spent many happy moments in that home. The ashram looked like it was in Metro magazine. Ma's art on the walls and the red leather couches were nothing like what I had expected. It was meticulous and beautiful, and I felt at home. The spiritual vibes were very strong.

This weekend was like a vacation compared to the service work we did in the communities. On another visit, I went to an audio Darshan with Ma that came through from Florida. I was surrounded by Italians, and several were Calabrians who looked like my relatives and were very friendly and happy for me to be there. That sealed it. I was ready to move to New York, even if only part-time.

Afterwards, we had Prasad (blessed food). This food was fabulous compared to Atlanta. There was pizza and eggplant parmigiana from the Bronx and desserts. I was ready to send for my clothes. I was in Heaven.

I learned so much during my time in New York and had fun while doing it. As I got to know him, I began to learn so much about myself. He helped me forgive myself. After Paul, I said I would never fall in love with a gay man again. Well, knowing him and spending time with him, there I was, falling in love with another gay Italian man, a Swami of all things.

I knew Achariya Das loved me, and he took very good care of me. It was truly fabulous, honest to God, one of the most fabulous times in my life. Living in an Ashram and doing the work was a prayer in motion. I have always cared about the people in the streets, and when I look into their eyes and see the void and feel the pain behind it, I have sobbed uncontrollably. The work and studies I did there were amazing, and I was in love with so much around me! Also, being around lots of Italians was the best thing! It was very hard in Atlanta to find Italians who were from Philly or New York. I had lost my Grandmother Stella right before that and I realized how much I missed her and so much of my daily life in Philly. The home I grew up in never felt the same after she passed, and I still longed to have all my family nearby. Most of all, I missed her arms around me, sitting with my grandmother, even as an adult, laying on the bed talking to her. I did that from a little girl. Sometimes, as a lesbian, it was really hard asking girlfriends to lay with me and hold me. Now, gay men are totally different.

I grew up always serving because that's how my grandfather Lou was, always giving to the needy and poor. And I really had been serving in Philly mostly with women and children. I learned so much more. I learned how to take care of the big statues called Murtis like the Ganesh, the elephant God, and Ma Durga, the compassionate goddess. I learned how to dress them, feed them, and pray to them. This was all new to me and yet it wasn't. When I was little, I would be punished in the convent by them putting me in the dark room where they had kept the big statues of Christ and Mary, which totally freaked me out and scared me. That was supposed to teach me how to be quiet! Not. But now, being around these big Murtis of gods and goddess was a pleasure and a new learning experience. Plus, I got to go to the Indian stores that sold these humongous brass statues that came from India. Some were bigger than two of me.

I had the most amazing experience with the Murti of Ma Durga. I never believed in any of the dressing the gods and goddess and feeding them, etc. So, there was this big Mother Durga Murti riding a lion, a symbol of power and protection. It was in the front room where we meditated. It was just phenomenal. I would sit in front of it and sometimes as soon as I got there, I would just sob. One woman would even sleep in front of it, and I asked one time if I could sleep in front of it, but I was not allowed at first but when I finally did, it opened up my heart and took away a lot of my grief and pain. It was a very moving experience.

I was living at the ashram in New York for a few years. I had some amazing contact with Ma. I had started my makeup line, Adita Cosmetics, while living there. I remember I gave Ma some of the products with my name on it, tape and paper because I didn't have it labeled yet. At like 6:00 a.m. in the morning, she had Achariya Das wake me up to tell me how much she loved it and to see if I could get something she used made for her. I think she was more excited than I was at times. She would tell everyone she was my manager, and it was so good. She was so funny, like a cross between Mother Teresa and Joan Rivers, honest to God. I was totally embraced by her, and by being at the house in New York, we became closer. I got to know a lot of the swamis and devotees from years before. There were hundreds of people to get to know. And the names, oh, my God, so many Krishnas and Anjanis.

I was the only one to get the name Idita. I ended up asking Ma if I could change the I to an A—Adita. I think I was probably the only one to have the balls to ask the Guru to change a letter and that was because I thought it looked better on the cosmetics label and it comes up first online. Ma teased me at first and said, "I name you "Elaine Parmigiana." No, Ma, please." Ma laughed and said, "I name you 'Idita Jaya.'" Ma said Idita is a Goddess to be praised and a Goddess who loves God and all the other Gods and Goddesses and Jaya means victory.

I learned a lot and loved going all over New York to revisit the places I had loved as a child, including Queens, Brooklyn, Coney Island, and many other towns and places. And oh, the food! One time, Ma said to Achariya Das, "She really doesn't love you. She loves the food that you eat." And everybody was laughing. A little ego killing, yeah? That's how it was with Ma. Sometimes she would play with you and sometimes it was a little ego death in there or sometimes a very big ego death that some of us struggled with but eventually totally embraced. You'd have to understand that afterwards you would look lighter and brighter when all that darkness was lifted from you.

I loved living with Acharaya because we went to places I had never been, like Brighton Beach. There were restaurants with caviar in the windows and Russian, Ukrainian, and Polish foods. The whole neighborhood was very European. The window displays also were draped with crystal trays and chandeliers. There was all this caviar. So, we went in, and we bought all kinds of stuff. We had a history of eating from the first day I ever went there. Most of our days were spent picking up food and waiting for deliveries, and on other days we went out to homes, hospitals, and to deliver food on the streets. To this day, I have never seen anybody serve like him. We got coats for the kids, backpacks, enough food for the families for a week, and school supplies. Also, at the long-term hospitals, where men and women had different diseases, we went to these places with carts stacked with toys, or in the case of adults, we brought flowers and Valentine's gifts and all kinds of stuff for them. Seeing the joy on the people's faces, it was so beautiful that sometimes I would cry.

True to my nature, one day as I was getting in the van to go out for deliveries, I was all dressed up and Achariya Das said, "Where do you think you're going today? To the salon?" I was all dressed up most of the time. Hey, I was in New York and a lot of times we stopped at some restaurants or, you know, stores, especially in Brooklyn.

I would go there for two weeks or so then go back to Atlanta to take care of my clients. I rented out my spare room in my home to make the money to help pay my mortgage, but I went through a lot of money in the nearly two years I did this. Eventually, we needed to figure out something more sustainable. "Okay, Okay," he said. "We will figure something out." We both had to get our blessing from Ma for me to move to the house. Ma said, "I'm going to let you go there to see how you get along, but if you come back with one extra pound on you, I will have you move out." I did not want to live by all the rules of the ashram house, as usual, yet I knew I wanted to live there and serve the world with this person. I wanted to be part of this organization that helped people.

I learned that we had a refuge for women and babies with AIDS set up in Uganda and a school in India. We provided food, medicine, education, and other means of support. What he decided to do was blow out the roof in the attic and create a whole apartment with a private bathroom, beautiful sunlit bedroom, and a kitchen area all for my use. Everyone else had a space more or less the size of a walk-in closet and paid a monthly rent. I did, too, but I had my own space that was gorgeous, and I was able to decorate the way I wanted. If I ever complained about anything, he would refer to me as the "princess and the pea." Some of the Swamis and my friends called it the Taj Mahal.

These years changed my life and world in a way that worrying about having the highest prestige meant nothing compared to helping those on the streets. Helping people who had nothing and even working for the seniors did something to my heart and soul that no amount of money could buy. Every day we went out on the streets. We'd load up the van the minute he woke up. He'd make hot chocolate and coffee and put that in these restaurant-sized containers, and we would take them down to the truck. We packed it with all kinds of food.

Then we would go pick up more stuff at this place in Brooklyn that donated all these boxes that they wanted to get rid of. Things like pretzels and candy, and we would bring all that back to the ashram. He turned his two-car garage into a sort of warehouse. He has turned the whole house into that now from what I hear. He fed the people who came every week, and we would make bags with sandwiches, snacks food, all of it. They would get enough to sustain them for a week.

One day, while deeply in meditation, I realized that I had never forgiven myself for being with Paul for 16 years. Loving another gay man, I was able to forgive myself and be at peace finally. I got to see all the great qualities that I loved about my relationship with Paul in Achariya Das. He was amazing for all the services he started, and he made me laugh like crazy. He liked the arts and movies. I liked doing many of the same things in New York that he did. We cooked together often when I was in Queens and loved the same kind of food. He was a highly educated person. He was and still is a powerhouse, a force to be reckoned with in New York. He's unbelievable in all the things he does.

When Achariya Das returned from living in California, he moved in with his mother and his niece. They began baking cookies for the homeless. After he lost his mother, he took his inheritance and bought a home big enough to support the growing, multi-faceted ashram. What started with homemade cookies has now expanded into this impactful, far-reaching charity that aims to break the cycle of poverty. The mainstay of this organization has always been the amazing volunteers who come out week after week to bag food and go out and serve the poor. He is always giving everything he's got. He and The River Fund have provided college scholarships to those in need. He gets up in the morning, goes to the gym, and after that, it's full speed ahead all day long.

I was under his domain and care, following his way of living and teaching. I was working with him almost every day doing some form of service. We laughed most days. Who wouldn't want to be with him? I freelanced doing hair in the city. I had several boutique owners in the Meat Packing District as clients and others that had been referred by clients in Atlanta and Philly. I didn't want to get a full-time job because I was committed to learning this way of life and all that I could from him.

One of the things I did when I was there was slicing cold cuts for sandwiches for people living on the streets. My besties, Pat, Sharon, and my Godkids, Danny and Sophie, came to visit for my birthday. I took them into the garage to see the food packing operations, supplies, toys, coats, and lots of everything to support these families. Danny and Sophie loved it, and yet I could tell their moms, my besties were not very happy. On the way to the Italian restaurant, Sharon was flipping out. They felt that after all the years of growth and therapy I had gone through, it was nuts for to me to spend so much of my time and money in New York, working in a three-car garage that was outfitted to look like a very nice warehouse. There were industrial refrigerators and freezers to keep our supplies.

When they saw me with Achariya Das, totally in love with him, I think they were worried about my relationship with him and the whole ashram. They acted like I didn't have enough sense to know what I was doing. And even though they were very protective of me, it was very reminiscent of my family's dynamic around my career. "After all the work you've done to heal, you're going to work in a garage?" My answer was, "Yeah, this work, this living here, has taught me so much and is so enriching." While I had served all my life, this work was awakening my love for humanity and deepening my spiritual connection. "It's been one of the best parts of my life." It was truly fabulous; honest to God, one of the most fabulous times in my life getting closer and closer to my Guru Ma.

Many of the Swamis had been with Ma for a very long time right from the beginning, and they were very devoted. And they loved me and my outgoing personality. So right away, I was in with all the old timers learning from them and with them. I felt so much love that it was lifting the years of pain and grief. From the start of me going to the New York Ashram it accelerated my move forward. Ma told me she was training me to be a spiritual teacher, and I would be funny just like her. Here in Atlanta, Swami Jaya Devi taught me a lot about love and tenderness. As the bitterness from the years behind me rolled off and out of me, I started feeling the effects of the yoga, meditation, chanting, and the power of the Guru.

All the Ashrams had their own little vibe. It was an Interfaith Teaching. In Florida, there were many Temples to honor different faiths and religions. It was also a Kali teaching. The Hindu goddess Kali is associated with power and transformation. She is widely worshiped in India. She is a complex goddess as she represents the destructive forces of time and the nurturing, gentle aspects of a mother. Kali protects her devotees and guides them toward liberation. Kali's presence can challenge your ego and force you to confront your own illusions! I loved the Kali teachings because I always had issues thinking Mother Mary was meek and mild. I felt that was how my grandmother Stella was and my grandmother Sue from Brooklyn, and, of course, Ma was more like Kali. So, when I experienced Kali in my life, I felt like she was my Goddess. Later in my spiritual life, I had a deep connection to Mother Mary and could feel the quiet strength of Her gentle approach, which was very similar to my Grandmother Stella.

A Long-Term Dream Comes True: Adita Cosmetics is Born

Every time I've gone through a breakup, I seem to always start a new business venture. After Callie, I started my collection of rental properties and then decided to focus on something I always wanted to do—have my own makeup and cosmetics line. My mom had been great at her craft and her gifts spilled over to me. I knew makeup inside and out. For years, I had been looking up cosmetic companies. I was working at the Ritz, and we carried a very exclusive makeup line. One day, cases of product were delivered, and I recognized the name on the box. It was actually one of the manufacturers I was interested in using. So, there was my answer.

I looked up the company and called them. They also had a space where potential buyers and marketers came for classes. I took a friend and coworker who was going to help coordinate the look. She was a hair stylist like me and did very beautiful soft makeup and liked different color palettes than me, so we made a great team. I met an instructor there named Lori Neapolitan who is one of the top educators in the world and does many fashion shoots. We immediately bonded, and I hired her as a consultant. I was so happy Lori took me on as a client to help me figure things out to create my line. Ma was totally smitten by the line. As I was creating it, Ma was doing some of the testing of creams and skincare potions.

I started my makeup line while living between New York and Atlanta. I had done makeup events through most of my career, whether it was to promote Sebastian's line or to do makeup for salon competitions, marketing videos, and the shows we put on in Philly and New York. I loved so many aspects of the cosmetology industry and even though I am an artist, I always needed the business side and marketing aspects.

Hair has always been my main means of income. I go a little crazy when people have no knowledge of the kind of money we bring in and make. If I felt that someone was unaware, I totally let them know that even back in the 70s and 80s, I had friends who were knocking out hair, making easily upwards of six figures. And I have friends who made $350,000 a year. If you work in a prestigious salon that supports your having two or three assistants, you can easily bring in $3,000-$5,000 a day or more. Others have become millionaires like a few of my former bosses. I liked my family and play time more than being concerned with making $20,000 a month. And yet, between my career and real estate and my inner drive, I have done pretty well.

So, the cosmetics line was a new venture. I loved it, and it was a lot of fun. Once again, I met a lot of interesting people, stars, and royalty. Adita Cosmetics was born under the name my guru gave me. I was fortunate to have the line in two salons in Nashville and two in Atlanta. One of my favorite things I got to do was work on two young, beautiful women who were going for the TV show "Next Top Model." One from Atlanta went on one show and did not like it and became a music star and the other beauty was from Nashville.

A friend of mine was the granddaughter of the Bush Bean family. She hired me to go for weeks to Nashville and work with her niece, and then I got connected to the modeling agency and put on fashion shows and shoots for these girls. Some of it happened at the Brentwood Country Club. I got involved with their events and had Adita Cosmetics doing special events for their members. I loved it. Meeting famous musicians, their wives, and the writers and producers was exciting. My aunt Marian loved country music, so while I was working, I put my phone on speaker and let her listen. I loved all that and sometimes I would stay at a hotel for the week or at the family's home. The people were so gracious and loving to me. In no time, I had the moms of the models coming to me and doing their hair and selling them products. I was like a one-woman event in myself. I had already travelled in the Nashville area back when Lynn was at Vanderbilt and now, I was getting to see areas and drives I had never done.

Francine the Queer and My Acceptance

In Atlanta, I got involved in the whole trans community and started doing big events with them. Some events had up to 700 people, and that was really a joy and almost like an act of service. While promoting my line, every year I got busier and busier and have two of my goddaughters come to help me and even travel with me to events in other areas. I hired makeup artists also. These events had so many different workshops and companies that hired LGBTQ folks. Several doctors who worked with the trans community came to the events, including a few from Europe and other places in the US. I did classes and worked with some famous surgeons and voice coaches and was on a panel with several of these people to help the patrons learn how to take care of their skin. I loved it all!

I also worked with private clients in my hotel room. I have always loved cutting wigs from when I was a young girl. I could knock out a haircut in 15 minutes and make these people look gorgeous. I would tape their face to feminize them and, of course, I would use Adita Cosmetics on them. When they looked in the mirror, some would just sob at how beautiful they looked and how they had hidden themselves for so long and could only do it on the sly. The ones who came from these very small towns where they risked death just tore me apart. One person, after I fixed her up, I said, "Oh my God, you look like Jane Fonda." She started crying and said, "Everyone always told my sister she looked like Jane Fonda and now I look like both of them." I felt so much compassion for them.

My goddaughters, Celestine and Margo, were awesome and learned a lot. I loved having my family with me. This went on for a number of years. I developed a very nice clientele and shipped out lots of products. It was difficult to get above a certain level.

No matter if the cosmetics are high end or low end, you need at least $500,000 for marketing. I didn't want to take on investors for several reasons that were scary to me, and it was the beginning of another huge transformation in my life that seemed more important than anything else.

Down at our ashrams in Atlanta, Florida, New York, and LA, Ma loved my skincare line so much that she wanted me to put it out at major events. She was amazing and wonderful in how she promoted Adita Cosmetics at every opportunity. I knew Ma loved me and wanted the best for me to go to the next level. I would need investors, and I also knew from Lori, my consultant, how hard it was to grow bigger. It's challenging, even in small boutique stores, to compete with companies like Laura Mercier and Bobby Brown. Even at our LA Ashram, there were so many interesting people coming to the workshops and seminars and several who are very famous wanted to get me to work in film. I always thought it was glamourous, but that wasn't my thing.

I did have several people who wanted to invest, but I just didn't want to do that. It's all about the marketing and visibility. It was and is a great experience and I still love it. I was happy with the salons who were carrying it, and I loved helping the Trans community. I have private clients and maybe a few events a year.

Meanwhile Back at the Ranch

I was so elated with my newfound spiritual life and embracing all the teachings at the Ashram. I took the yoga teacher training most of all because I wanted to learn from Ma. Our Ashram is interfaith, and there was so much to learn. I soaked it all up. The second reason was that I really wanted to do children's yoga, and I did so at a shelter for abused kids.

The Atlanta ashram had their own expectations of the way I was to behave in order to get closer to Ma. The group there was much younger than me and were more focused on formalities when it came to relating to the leadership, rather than authenticity. There were a lot of rules at the Atlanta ashram, and I was never great with rules, especially coming from young, non-Italians. That's the way I was raised, so it was very hard for me to take orders from them. While I always knew how to approach with respect, the forced formality always felt like a barrier to being my true self. And yet, when I needed to be proper, I knew how to handle myself. I was often chosen to be a part of special ceremonies involving guest teachers and leaders from other countries.

I was asked to teach at another yoga studio in Atlanta. The Kashi CEO told me that just because I inquired about teaching elsewhere, I would never be allowed to teach at Kashi. I felt he was spiritually bullying me, and I wrote a letter telling him and some of the leadership just how I felt. I knew to teach at Kashi you had to sign a non-compete clause. That was not going to happen. In fact, I left a fabulous salon here in Atlanta because they wanted me to do the same. I was certainly not doing it at Kashi.

I wasn't having any of their little games here in Atlanta. After I became a resident at the New York Ashram, Achariya Das saw how they treated me. I was there for a week for a work study and some of the Swamis asked that my work service be to cook for the people in the first Kali Natha Yoga Teacher Training with Ma. Of course, I was beyond thrilled. Oh My God! Some of the Atlantans tried to intimidate me, but I had my own little team. My attitude was "fuck off, I got this" and I did. That week I made all kinds of Italian vegetarian dishes, especially my fried eggplants and eggplant parmigiana. Everyone was happy, especially Achariya Das and Swami Laxman Das, except he complained that I forgot to put bowls of marinara for dipping. I had a great time with all my favorites that were there, especially the LA swamis and Achariya Das.

I was staying at Shirdi House and didn't know the house rules there when Swami Jaya Devi was there with her entourage. At the end of the week, I was totally exhausted and started not feeling well. That night after dinner when everything was cleaned up, I had fixed myself a plate and was sitting in the kitchen eating and talking to another resident. Suddenly, some Atlanta ashram people came in and were emphatically waving at me to get up. I was unclear about what they wanted. Apparently, I was supposed to get up and Pranam to Jaya Devi and take my food outside to eat. This was not a rule I knew or was used to. I was really exhausted from cooking all day, so I'm not sure if I had known, I would've met their expectations. In a way, I felt like they should've been Pranaming to me after all my hard work.

I got really perturbed over the way they treated me. Let's say, Philly Italian perturbed. I was rooming with several people from the Atlanta Ashram. The next morning, on the advice of a friend, I went to the doctor and was diagnosed with bronchitis and had to be put on steroids. I had to stay in bed for a few days. One of the Swamis that I hadn't known well took such excellent care of me that I'm still connected to her today. There was a big weekend event planned, but Achariya Das had to return to New York. I thought everyone in the house was at the event, but unbeknownst to me, there was someone in the bedroom next to mine. Achariya Das called me, and we had a loud, expressive conversation on speaker phone about my experiences. He was furious with the way they were treating me. I had no idea that someone had eavesdropped on our entire conversation and went back and reported it all to another Swami. Achariya Das apparently then called out the Atlanta Ashram leadership and heatedly expressed his concerns. He was a Swami, but under the orange cloth he wore, he was still the Italian gay boy from NY with a temper! Somehow it all got to Ma. I really did not know what went on.

The next weekend a friend told me he didn't look too good after coming down from Ma's Rooms. I didn't hear from him for a few weeks. I assumed he was busy. I was scheduled to go to New York, but before that I had some eye surgery. My friend Linda called me, and said, "D called me to see how you were." "What?" I said. "Why didn't he just call me?" I began to think that he didn't care about me anymore. When I went to New York, it was really weird. When he picked me up, he seemed distant, but I didn't know why. When we got back to the house, he explained that things had changed and he had to focus more on his work. I had loved us being together. It was mostly all about service, yet we made it fun and always laughed and enjoyed each other's company. I wasn't used to this business-only Achariya Das.

Much later I learned that he wasn't allowed to call me or anyone anymore unless it had to do with business. I was used to having contact with him several times a week.

One day in the car, we got into a heated argument. "I might sell this building and move into a one-bedroom apartment. I might get out of this whole thing," he said. "Oh, really? And you want me to sell my condo and move here and do that when you don't even know what you're doing?" was my reply. We were getting loud. We stormed into the house. One of our people was cleaning and was setting up the meditation room, and we scared them with our yelling.

I began to think I had stayed there long enough. One of the biggest reasons I wanted to be there was because whenever Ma came to New York to do workshops, she would stay at the house. And, of course, I totally loved Achariya Das and being with him. I loved going to teach both yoga and meditations. Sometimes when Ma was there, she would call up to my room and talk to me. She gave me advice when I started my makeup line, and she supported me around my book. We had so much to talk and laugh about. Ma's husband was Italian. So, I got close to her in many ways that most people never got the chance to do. I didn't think I could ever get that close to her anywhere else. I was opening up for all good things to come my way.

Even though I had furnished my condo, I didn't stay there and decided to stay in Atlanta. I was not into the freezing weather anymore. I had already bought three properties in Florida and the money I made with the properties funded my living and being in New York, keeping my house in Atlanta, and going back and forth to Florida and New York.

Learning from Ma, Becoming Adita

From all of this, what I have learned is that I have constantly been looking for love. I've been looking for someone to love me unconditionally. I had to learn to love myself in that way. Ma gave me more unconditional love than anyone ever had. She was the epitome of love, and I'd never felt that in anyone. She gave me many teachings. Depending how you were able to take them in made a big difference in your growth. One big teaching that changed my life that I'm so grateful for was that Ma always knew what you needed even before you were aware of it. There were weekend intensives, and we would all gather in the Temple. One of those times Ma called me up, I wasn't sure where it was going to go and sometimes things didn't always make sense until you let it seep in. This time, Ma very emphatically said, "Adita, I don't want you EVER to let anyone shame you or call you names" and then the finger came out, and she said, "NOT EVEN YOU, Adita!" Wow! I had so many great years with Ma and at the Ashram. This changed so much of the way I allowed people to talk to me. It opened me up in so many ways.

I never knew I was an empath, and yet, I knew I was totally connected to source and never claimed it because it actually scared me. One of the times Ma was doing an Intensive in NY, I felt my whole throat chakra opening up. My ears, which are part of that, popped and I started hearing in a very different way. It was very hard when I went back to work. I suddenly learned I was clairvoyant and clairaudient. I was finally understanding how psychics can do readings over the phone. Everyday my life was changing for the better and the awareness I felt was amazing. The closer I got to Ma, the more I realized her power to help us change. There are a lot of fabulous spiritual teachers out there, but Ma was my perfect fit. And she taught with so much humor I always said she was a cross between Bette Midler and Mother Theresa. Ma always seemed to know what each of us needed.

There is a reading in the Big Book of AA that states, "If we are painstaking about this phase of our development, we will be amazed before we are halfway through, we are going to know a new freedom and new happiness." My life was clearly on that path, and the Ashram has taken me the rest of the way.

In the Fall of 2011, Ma was not feeling well, and her back was really hurting her. She suffered with pain a lot in her life and was confined to a wheelchair in her earlier years. Yoga changed that for Ma. Ma's main caretaker called me in November and told me about Ma's pain. For me, I had seen it in her face at the Atlanta Intensive in October. I told myself it was exhaustion. She was asking me for suggestions.

Sometimes, I'm the best one to ask and sometimes I'm not. Through my own friends, family, clients, and those of other stylists, I know some of the best experts in many fields. My wife would say, "She has a posse of her own," and she also was very funny and said, "They control my life!" People come to me a lot to ask me about their aches and pains.

Because I had a grandfather and mother who were hypochondriacs, I will analyze all the things that are mentally or emotionally wrong with them or where they are holding their grief, anger, rage, and whatever else in their body. That's how I do my diagnoses.

Now, even though I have no medical degree whatsoever, I sometimes feel like a medical intuitive. I cannot claim that, but I know lots of people who are. My acupuncturist is the best, and I am not allowed to give his name out anymore. I've sent him so many clients, and he wants to retire. Knowing that Ma had recently faced a traumatic betrayal, I suspected that she was carrying a lot of grief and sorrow from that experience.

Ma kept putting the pain on hold. She wanted to be there for her beloved grandson, Tony, and Ximena's wedding. It was a grand affair at the Ashram and Ma wouldn't miss a thing. Ma, at that point, was in her 70s and still teaching yoga and traveling to Atlanta, Los Angeles, New York, and more. Then, there was Christmas! The setting on the Ashram was like a Hallmark movie, being that it was on 68 acres with all the Ashram houses decorated and lit up. Ma had also opened a piece of land for members to build their own beautiful homes on the other side of the river. And she also gave land to build a beautiful, assisted-living facility for low-income people. Ma loved Christmas and seeing all the kids return home to the Ashram. Christmas Eve was amazing There was a private party for the kids of all ages and their parents, and I felt very happy to be a part of it. The toys and gifts just flowed for quite a few hours. And then Christmas Day was a big Italian feast. By then, almost everyone was there, and it was magical just like the Christmases I experienced in a small rowhome in South Philly.

Not only did we celebrate Christmas in a big way, but she also always taught a big New Years Intensive, and she was just funny as could be. Ma released her new book and for some reason she was showering me with so much love and attention that whole week and making us all laugh. Several of us loved buying her clothes and jewelry and designer bags. Ma was a dresser up to the end. The first day of the Intensive, Ma comes out to teach yoga in a bebe, hot pink yoga outfit that Skanda, another devotee, bought her. Ma preferred bebe to other yoga wear. She also had a gorgeous jacket and these long, hot pink feather earrings that I bought her intertwining with her long dark locks of hair.

Then she hollers out, "Adita, Swami Krishnabai came in to check on me. She took one look at me and said Ma where are you going dressed like that, you look like Michael Jackson." All said in her Brooklyn accent. She raised her hand to show us her gloves. I bought her these black lace fingerless gloves that had a rhinestone broach with feathers shooting out. Everybody started clapping and Ma gave me a big grin.

And that was the magic of Ma! Most of the time she would have us laughing before we went into that very deep state. I have tried many different teachings and teachers over the years, yet Ma was it for me. I needed her, she could make me laugh and scream, and in the next moment bring you into your deepest self. Ma got her diagnosis right after New Years, and it was pancreatic cancer. I kept seeing the number 4. I was hoping it was 4 or 40 years. With her first dose of chemo, it basically took her down.

Ma died 4 months later. People were coming in from everywhere and gathering in the Ashram and went upstairs to see her alive for the last time. I was late, so by the time I got there I had to wait until the morning to see her. The sobs and hysterics that came out of me… I felt like my insides were going to come out. I never remembered crying like that before. People were still flying in from all over, and we were all trying to comfort each other. I also knew I wanted to be there in the kitchen to greet and serve as Satsang came in from everywhere. Ma's memorial at the Ashram was like a sea of white. There were rabbis and well-known spiritual teachers from many other traditions who came to honor her and tell stories about how she changed their lives. Ma was world-renowned for her service to the world. It still amazes me how Ma, a poor woman from Brooklyn, created centers, schools, orphanages, and Ashrams in some of the worst parts of the world. Talk about dedication, teachings, and tenacity. There are many books and teachings written by Ma that you can find online. While Ma was alive, she received so many awards from around the world, and here in Atlanta, I was there for a few of them.

Thank God! We all had each other to lean on. We also had different nights where we got on Ma's meditations through Zoom, and we had time to get together and comfort each other.

From MAFIA PRINCESS *to* LESBIAN CHIC

CHAPTER 14

THE BIGGEST GODDESS OF ALL

When I met my wife, Nina, it was like she was infused with Ma. It was the relationship I had waited for my entire life. Nina embodied all the good stuff that I was missing and craving from my family minus the pain.

I was back in Atlanta full time and was no longer going back and forth to New York. It took me some years to process losing Ma on earth. I was really lonely at that point, so I began going out on dates, but I met no one very interesting. Finally, I joined two dating sites. I went on several dates, and a few were very nice but not interesting enough to go on a second date.

Right before I met Nina on Zoosk, I went out with this woman for just one brief encounter. She was at a bowling alley that night that happened to be near where I worked, and I was coming from work to meet her, so I was dressed up with big rhinestone hoops and, of course, with all my Adita Cosmetics on. Yet I was dressed like that my whole life. One of the boons gurus can give you is that after learning from them, I was able to see through people, to see where their darkness was in their body and the light as well. I walked into the bowling alley, and this woman who was very pretty yet looked totally empty inside almost like a skeleton. I already knew that she had just gotten done taking care of both of her parents with Alzheimer's. I really wanted to walk past her. It kind of scared me.

She was the only woman in there. It was a gay men's bowling league, so I couldn't go anywhere. I stuck out like a sore thumb. She didn't live near me, and I didn't have that many nights off because I was so busy. I canceled some dates I had around the corner for coffee because I kept myself so busy. It just so happened that she was going to be right where I worked that night. She said, "Why don't you come to the bowling alley? I'll take a break, and we'll have something to drink or whatever." When I walked in, obviously overdressed for bowling, I saw the look on her gay men's faces. I had to say hello and then noticed that she had on some sort of khaki pants and a denim shirt. I hate khakis. On the denim shirt pocket there was some sort of embroidery with cats and dogs on it. I noticed that right away, and I had to say something. "Oh, that's very nice. Did somebody do that?" "Oh, yeah, my friend did it," she said. *Great*, I thought.

I wanted to run out because nothing about this felt like something I would be interested in. I know she probably felt the same way. So that night I left, got in the car, and right away I wrote on Facebook, *"If I go out with one more lesbian that has five cats and three dogs, I might lose it."* I thought, *I'm going back to the gay Swami with the red leather couches and fabulous art.*

I went home and got onto my computer and checked out my messages on Zoosk. I had a wave from a woman named Nina. I looked at her picture, and I thought, *fuck, she's gorgeous, she's hot, she's sexy, and my type.* Then I saw she was from Philadelphia, and she knew I lived in Atlanta, but she didn't know I'm from Philly. So, I looked more at her profile and there was an honesty and vulnerability that I had not really experienced in others, even just in the way she looked. I read what she wrote in her profile and thought it was so real. If they said they loved camping and the great outdoors, I moved on. Nina did say she loved the beach and being in the ocean and I do too. Little did I know that she meant sitting in a great beach chair, going to the bar on the beach, not taking long walks at sunset!

I wrote back to her. I said, "Sorry. Um, three cats? I'm allergic. Cigarettes? I'm allergic." She was honest about her drinking, smoking, and financial troubles and that honesty and humility is really what got my heart. But I thought, *well, she's not for me, but maybe if she's from Philadelphia, she's got to know a lot of Philly lesbians and people I know.* She answered, "Well, if that's a deal breaker for you, so are bi women for me." Why I ever put bisexual on a women's dating site, I'll never know. Probably because I was still attracted to men.

So, we both gave each other the freaking finger, the Italian FU, or whatever. But then we came back to center, and she said, "Why don't we become friends on Facebook?" She was strong and not backing down in a very good way. My kind of person already. We talked a little bit, and it turned out that every part of our life, from when I was a child, in some way we were connected. She grew up in South Philly, in Drexel Hill. I spent a lot of time there growing up with my Aunt Connie and Uncle Fred.

When she came out, she was living with her first Italian partner around the corner from my best friend. And not only that, when I had been exploring my identity and I hung out on 10th and Snyder with most of the lesbians from High School, she came by there. One of her besties lived right there and her dad owned Willy's Pizza. After I got to know her, I totally remembered her. She was older than me, and she had gotten out of this big convertible with some other women. I remember thinking she looked kind of butch. She was dressed fabulous, and we locked eyes. I remember feeling something but just let it go because it scared the hell out of me. I didn't know, because I still liked guys, and she kind of scared me, not because she was dangerous, but because I was not in my own power back then. As we talked, I started to put all that together.

She lived around the corner from me in Center City as well. We went to the same clubs and restaurants. We decided to become friends on Facebook, and no joke, when I put her name in, seven people I knew popped up as mutual connections. One of her best friends, Bernadette, was a close colleague of mine, and she was connected to my two ex-bosses, Mare and Ro. She knew my cousin Toni, my sister Sadie's godmother, and her two daughters. How did I ever miss her?

And so, we started talking, and I just liked her a lot. Susie Q always would say to me even as a child that I should work for the FBI because I was so inquisitive and now here I was doing my own search from my Facebook Friends, looking into the people that I date. I called my people in Philly, one who was her best friend, Bern, who said, "She's the most beautiful person inside and out." And then I called Mare and Ro, my former bosses, because I knew they had a great relationship and been together for years. I said, "She seems so strong minded." Rose replied, "If anybody could handle her, you're the one." They were right because I did stand up to her. Before you knew it, we were having phone dates and all that good stuff.

What really attracted me to her, at the beginning, was her humbleness on her profile on Zoosk. She told the truth. "I've experienced the highs of life, and I've lost my fortune, but I am okay with it," she wrote. Little did she know, I was going through something similar as my real estate investments were tanking. That day, I had just cut off all my hair and went blonde. I was very happy with my new look. I was with a friend who always made me giggle. I was in one of the best Italian restaurants in Atlanta and even though Italians don't drink cappuccino after dinner, I do and the way I was holding my cup with my finger out made an impression on her while she was looking on Zoosk. A friend of mine took my picture and I was, of course, all dressed to the nines, looking great. Nina was very attracted to that photo. We talked every night from that point on.

Finally, she invited me to Philly for New Year's Eve, but I didn't go. We decided she would come to Atlanta in January. She was coming for three or four days, and we said that if it doesn't work out, I had an extra bedroom, or she could go to a hotel. She came to visit Decatur, but while she was at the airport, something happened, she missed her plane, and she was looking at her Facebook. I had posted a picture of Ma, my guru, and she told me she couldn't stop crying when she saw that picture. And she said to me, "Who is this woman?" That's my Guru Ma," I answered. "It's taking my breath away," she said. "I can't stop crying." Immediately I knew we were meant to be together.

I knew right then and there, because of the way other people in the ashram and the world meet their gurus. I said, "There's some meaning behind this whole thing with Ma."

I picked her up at the airport, and the minute I laid eyes on her, she looked like my whole family in one. She was beautiful, like my Aunt Marian. She had this big fur coat on. She was classy and magnetic. And that is exactly what I mean, I loved her energy. She had highs and lows. She was brilliant. Nina was an entrepreneur in the fresh roasting coffee and food industry before it was trendy and a big part of our lives. She went on to become what a friend called an accidental banker and worked on Wall Street. A friend asked her to help her out at the bank, and she didn't really want to, but she kept getting promoted higher and higher in the banking industry. She had a level of sophistication and was magnetic. Nina worked at a well-known investment brokerage firm, Butcher and Singer, that was strictly male-dominated. She worked with very wealthy clients who she wined and dined with. Then her mother and father both got sick, and she stopped working to take care of them.

Anyway, I picked her up, and I had a little velvet mini skirt on with a lace top, and the minute she got in the car, it was like heaven to me. Something felt like she was my spouse that I hadn't seen for many years, my long, lost soulmate. She was supposed to stay for three or four days, and she ended up staying for 11. That was it for us. I knew when she walked in and through my house that Ma had sent her.

I took her to the ashram in Florida, and no matter where I took her, people swooned over her. All the straight people in the salon that were from Alpharetta, just swooned over her when she came to the salon. They invited her to these parties that I never wanted to go to. She just had that kind of personality. So much so that one of the girls I worked with got a little crazy. Nina was at the salon getting her hair done, and she was laying back at the shampoo bowl. I was busy working. She was going to get her hair cut. And all of a sudden, I noticed that I couldn't see the shampoo bowl, but everybody was looking over there. One of the ladies that worked next to me, her face looked in disbelief. I heard Rosita, our assistant, say to Naomi, "You better not let Elaine see you do that. You know what's going to happen."

I stopped doing my client to see what was going on and there was Naomi laying on Nina while she was back in the chair getting a shampoo with her head on Nina's shoulder. Nina had that effect on people. She was like Ma inside, which I discovered more and more. And so, I don't know if it was a spiritual thing. I don't know what it was, but oh, my God, I just went beyond crazy. I said, "You better get the fuck off of her." My wife would never come back to the salon because everybody would congregate around her. Everybody loved her.

Nina had a house in Fishtown, in one of the hottest selling neighborhoods Philly. They were opening up banks in that area. During the 2008 bank fallouts, Nina had lost her big job in New York. She went to work for a bank there in the marketing department to bring in the local businesses. She got all the businesses to come to that bank in Philly. She was in the marketing department and after they got all these accounts, they let go of the whole marketing team. So once again, at 60 years old, she lost her job. Then she got hired by another bank, and she got all those people to leave and come with her to Hyperion Bank.

Anywhere we went out to eat in her neighborhood, everybody knew her. She put on these big events in Fishtown to get all the people and businesses to come together. The huge, green, urban park was encircled by the many restaurants and cool shops.

People love her still today. When she died, I can't tell you how many people wrote to me, called me, said she was responsible for teaching them, and that if it wasn't for her, they wouldn't know where they would be today. Men, women, everybody. She was a big deal. They asked her to be like a state representative, but she didn't want that. She didn't want them to go into some of her history.

After the going back and forth, she finally said she was willing to move. I was not moving, and I couldn't move because of my clients. It felt like everything happened all at once. She didn't know what she was going to do with her house, because it was undervalued. At that point, the market had dropped. She was still looking for another job because she was forced into early retirement, so she didn't get nearly what she was going to get for her retirement, and she had to wait until she was 62 to get that.

We didn't want to live together. I didn't want to live together because I have this thing about it, and I almost moved in with Callie. I told her, "No way. I want to know you for six months." I was not moving out of my house for anybody or having anybody move in with me. Then suddenly, everything fell together. My neighbor, Carol, two doors down built a townhouse and redid the whole thing. She held it for Nina for five or six months. She was very generous, and it didn't matter to her. She didn't want to show any income anyway. And so, then Nina's boss said, "Can I move in your townhouse? I'm breaking up with my husband." She took over Nina's house and fixed everything up that needed fixing. And then Nina just moved here to Carol's townhouse. Easy peasy.

She had three cats, and she smoked and drank some. It was everything I said I did not want. I should have known that lesson, "Don't say what you don't want. Ask for what you want." So, she came here to Atlanta, and it was just magical with her. I took her to the Ashram, and it used to be that I would cook all the time there. I would do a lot of things for them and soon Nina was helping out as well. Nina got her spiritual name in only four months, which was Ma's name. Nina was highly, highly, highly spiritual. They adored her at the Ashram.

She started cooking for them, and all of a sudden, they preferred her food to mine, so she started cooking for everybody. She came from an Italian family. They were a little bit more high class and educated than my family. Her one uncle was a famous artist, like one of the greats from Italy. He was well known. Another uncle owned a factory. They were really brilliant people. And one of her uncles was actually a spiritual teacher who had met my guru, Ma, years earlier. And Nina remembered Ma's voice when she heard it.

Marriage: Gun License or Marriage License

Nina and I decided to get married but not live in the same house. One funny moment, where we went to get our marriage license in downtown Decatur, they offered both marriages licenses and gun licenses in the same room. Should we get both? We had planned a big wedding down at the ashram for my family, like 100 people, but they couldn't accommodate us for some reason. We ended up having a wedding at the house and it was supposed to be 25 people, but true to my nature about 70 people showed up. It was the most people we could fit in my home. I handpicked the people. Others were asking me if they could come, even offering to pay to attend the wedding. I couldn't invite everyone even though I wanted to. We had a band. We had Johnny, our best friend, who is an international entertainer, and Nina's best friend Andy, who's is a professional singer and actor. We took every bit of furniture out of the house and put up folding tables out on the patio. We even thought about tearing the wall down next door at my neighbors. My wife was just a saint for putting up with me. I guess, so is everybody else.

I had it catered from my favorite Italian restaurant with New York roots. The food was fabulous. The cake was so beautiful, it made me cry and Nina was perplexed. Our outfits were beautiful. We had them made from the Indian store. Nina wore a stunning jacket. The wedding was so deeply spiritual, and we had a lot of people from the ashram. They started the evening by chanting. We had our best friends from Philly here. My good friend, Alex, officiated. She's a Jewish girl from the suburbs of Philly often compared to the character Mrs. Maisel. She is hysterical and had us and our friends both laughing and crying throughout our sweet, emotional ceremony.

We had big life-size stand-up images of Dean Martin and Frank Sinatra, behind us. It really was magical. Both of us agreed it was the happiest day of our lives.

Nina knew what was going on in people's heads, what I was thinking, and what other people were thinking. It just came to her. One day I was at work, and I was telling my friend Naomi that I had a fight with Nina, and I was also telling her about our sex life, not our intimacies, but how great it was and all. When I went home, Nina asked, "Are you gonna tell Naomi everything about us?" "What are you talking about?" I asked. "Oh, I heard everything today," she said. "How did you hear what I said?" I was thinking, *did I leave my phone off the hook or something?* She said, "I can't help it. It comes to me, and there's nothing I can do about it."

Many years before, one of her uncles had and taught a spiritual group in his little house in the Italian market section. Her uncle taught her how to time travel. Nina had an abundance of Shakti, and I wasn't sure he taught her how to manage it. Nina vibrated at a higher level. When Shakti rises up your spine, you become more enlightened. It's Spiritual energy, and when I first felt it, it felt great. It can be scary if you have a teacher that raises it quickly. One time, I was so in ecstasy that it felt like a put my finger in an electric socket. That's not good. You need a teacher who knows what they are doing and can teach you to regulate your energy.

When Nina came here, it was the best thing for her. She fell in love with our Swami Jaya Devi, and she learned so much. And Nina was just brilliant, so deep and so loving, and so kind yet, if you saw her, you would never know that right away. She could clear a room with her temper, too. She was like a cannoli, strong on the outside and soft on the inside. So, we started going to the ashram and life was just beautiful until my cousin came along.

Family Déjà vu

It was Christmas, a time when I really missed my big, Italian family being together. Our cousin, who had been complaining about the trajectory of his life, wanted to move to Atlanta for a new start. I felt bad for him as he was always trying to figure out his life. I wasn't able to let him stay with me, but Nina took him into her home and over the course of a year, he completely wreaked havoc on our lives. It was just one sociopathic event after another. He brought a snake home which was poisonous and landed him in the hospital. He smoked pot around the neighborhood kids. He trashed a car. He spewed an endless list of lies. When asked to leave, he just produced excuse after excuse. Turns out he was probably hiding out from trouble back home.

After all the work I'd done and having finally found my true love, here I was again dealing with the kind of dysfunction I'd grown up with. I really did not want to deal with his craziness. We kept telling him to get out, but he wouldn't listen. All the drama was putting a strain on our relationship.

Eventually, after a neighborhood altercation, he started fighting with Nina. She finally reached her breaking point. The next day, Nina got up, packed all his stuff up really nice for him to take, and she put it on the porch. I would have fucking thrown it out the window in trash bags. When she called him at work, she said, "When you come home, be prepared. I packed all your stuff. You don't live here anymore." He rushed home and started fighting with her, pointing his finger in her face and recording their fight. She pushed him away. He told the cops that Nina scratched him, and they took her to jail for that.

I was on my way home, and by time I got home, Nina was gone. Thank God I got home after this all went down, and I didn't see them take her away, because I probably would have gotten taken in too. It really brought back all my PTSD around seeing my dad taken. I was so worried about Nina. My beautiful wife and her sense of pride and dignity for all the things she accomplished in this world was going to jail. This woman who had held some of the highest positions in places where she worked was in a jail cell.

It's so true what they say about being in there. She wasn't allowed her medications for seven days until her doctor approved. And they only got water two times a day, and once it was done, that was it. Luckily the two girls in her cell helped take rags with cold to put on her forehead because her blood pressure was spiking. And true to Nina's good heart, after I picked her up, we had to go to the bonds office to get those women out who took such good care of her. That was Nina through and through. Thank God she was only in there for two nights and yet I saw what it did to her.

The woman who owned the house and her mother helped our cousin find a place to stay to get him out of the neighborhood before Nina returned home. Dealing with the lawyers and aftermath of this altercation was incredibly stressful for us both.

Ding Dong the Witch is Dead

When Dad finally got out of jail, he didn't last much longer. He got sick and died within a few years. While he was in jail, they brought him over to North Carolina to go to Duke for heart surgery, so he was sick in jail as well.

My father always found a way to find me. I had a cell phone, but I wouldn't answer it if I didn't know the number. When he finally got out for the last time, he called my salon. We had a receptionist at the time, and she came back to me in the color room, and she said, "There's a gentleman that wants to speak with you." "Who is it?" I asked. "I don't know." So, I picked it up because it could have been a client. It was him. "Don't hang up on me. Don't hang up on me," he said. "I just want to tell you how much I miss you." I didn't even say a word. I just hung up. He was a conniver. He would tell anything to anybody when he wanted to get something from them. I'm sure he was using his girlfriend, Carol, at the time who was trying to help him get set up. Some women sadly seem to get some status from dating a gangster. Eventually, Dad had sold his house and moved into his parents' home. He wanted everyone who inherited part of my grandparents' home to officially sign away their rights. I had already washed my hands of that whole situation.

When I found out that he had died, I was at the doctor's office with Nina. My brother Louis called to tell me. Nina looked concerned and wanted to know what was wrong. I said that everything was great; my father died. She was astonished! I told her that I had planned to do the Mummers Strut when he died. She pleaded with me not to do that until we got home, but I couldn't help myself from dancing down the hall.

My World Starts to Crumble

After the situation with my cousin, I could see how much Nina was suffering from what happened. I wanted her to get some help with it, but she said she was fine, and I shouldn't worry. My intuition was so spot on, and I started to feel that Nina was ill. When Nina was younger, she had the old-fashioned bariatric surgery. When they did it the first time, a lot of people died. They basically reroute your whole stomach. So, she, had a lot of physical issues. She was older than I am. At the beginning of January, she had her physical which came back as clean as a whistle. About six weeks later, every night after dinner, she would have this pain that went around her whole stomach area, and her back. She thought, *well, maybe it's indigestion, maybe it's acid reflux, maybe it's this, maybe it's that.*

But when I took her to that appointment, honest to God, I said to myself, *something's going to happen here that my wife's going to die from.* I knew it. It's happened to me with my mom too. Like I said, I'm very intuitive. She was hurting her every night. I said, "Nina, you gotta go get this checked out." "Well, I just had every physical and they said everything was positive. They didn't find anything," she said. She had all her tests, and this went on for a month.

Finally, we we're headed to Florida soon. I said, "I am not driving down to Florida and have you get sick and go to a hospital in some small rural town. You either go find out what this is, or we're not going." And so, she went. Sure enough, they found a spot, and they said, "Go away. We're going to analyze this. We won't know for a while, at least for a few weeks."

When we got back, the doctor called us in and told us that Nina had something called cholangiocarcinoma. Most people have never heard of it, not even most doctors. They told us we needed to get to somebody very, very quickly. Now, me, I've always been known for finding the best doctors and experts in the area where I live. That's why I love the salons I work in, especially with my Jewish clientele. So, through my friend Naomi's client we found this doctor from MD Anderson in Texas. They're one of the top hospitals in the country.

We are so lucky to be living in Atlanta with three or four major hospitals. When they said she had that disease, they sent us to a surgeon, and he was fabulous, except it wasn't a surgeon that we needed. We really liked him a lot, and he did not mince words. He said, "You should have been getting chemo six months ago. Hopefully, you have six months to live, but I'm going to get you in with the best doctor here. I'm going to tell them you need chemo as soon as they could get you in." And that week, Nina started her chemo.

When we came home from that meeting, I went right up to my altar in my bedroom. I screamed and cried to Jesus, every saint there is, and I said, "Please just give us one more Christmas," because we loved Christmas. And we ended up getting two more Christmases. In between that, we had some of the best care. She almost died a few times. The first week of chemo is one of the worst weeks. My guru died from the chemo they gave her because it was too much. They told Nina she might die too, and my wife was not an easy patient at all.

And so, the first round of chemo she got, they said, "If anything happens, get her to hospital as quick as possible." Well, she wouldn't go. If I would have listened to her, she could have died because the chemo was too much for her system. There were a lot of hard times, and there were so many beautiful moments. We were still able to travel back and forth to the Florida Ashram. We rented our favorite house in Sebastian that had a beautiful private pool where we could see across to the river. Another favorite place of ours was Amelia Island, Florida. I managed to get a beautiful condo with a huge, gorgeous bed overlooking the Atlantic. I was afraid for us to go anywhere that wasn't close to fabulous teaching hospitals and Amelia Island was right near Mayo.

Very few people, including doctors, knew what cholangiocarcinoma was, not even my own cousin and doctor friends. It's cancer of the bile ducts. I think things have gotten slightly better, but most people die in the first 6 months. We were so lucky to have so many fabulous friends and family around us and the amazing love and prayers from all our Ashrams. The way everyone just loved on us was beyond beautiful. We were so spiritually lifted! We were held by our Higher Powers whether it was Jesus, the Buddha, or Ma. I always like to think it was all of them.

About a year in, she entered palliative care. She loved her doctor, a young gay man with an awesome personality who had studied at Sloan Kettering. He recommended a famous doctor from there who had just published a book on palliative care and when we met with him, he said, "Whatever they're doing in Atlanta, you have great doctors. I read all your records. You were given six months and it's already been a year since your diagnosis. The only thing I can tell you is to do yoga, meditation, and acupuncture."

I, of course, was a yoga teacher and taught meditation. I made sure as soon as we got back from New York, we found an acupuncturist. I believe that acupuncturist made her live another year. She started getting better and better, and then the acupuncturist left to visit her family in Korea for a month, and Nina started going downhill really quickly that month. She just couldn't eat and keep it down. We were starting to hear about Covid just as her acupuncturist came back from Korea and as soon as she had a treatment, she wanted to go eat at her favorite breakfast spot. She wanted Italian peppers and eggs on a sandwich roll. We were both so happy she could keep it down.

Soon after Covid hit, the acupuncturist couldn't see her anymore. I think if she could have continued to see her, Nina would have lived longer. I begged the acupuncturist and said I would pay her anything to treat Nina. She started to go downhill. I totally believe in acupuncture. Dr. Jolly is an amazing doctor, and he did a great job helping keep Nina alive. They tried one more round of radiation and it didn't help at all. She went into full blown hospice at home and thank God we were able to keep her at home. Covid was taking out so many lives. Even though Covid didn't kill Nina, I feel she was a casualty of it.

We had amazing love all around us. People said her death was as beautiful as our wedding. We had all these people singing, chanting, singing Italian songs. I mean, it just was beautiful.

Nina wanted her own funeral before she died, and she wanted us to go down to the ashram so she could die there. There was no way she could make it down to Florida. So, we had her in bed at home. She was hysterical, flirting with the nurses until the last minute here in her house. And we had people coming. A good friend, Mary Francis, sent big flowers, like funeral flowers. We had the room all fixed up. She got that second wind with people around saying she wanted a martini one night. She wanted a beer and a hot dog another night. We had everybody around us. It was unbelievable. Johnny and Mike, who started out as our neighbors, had already become our besties and were there night and day for us and so many other people helped, day in and day out. After Nina died, Johnny would come every day and feed me. He did my laundry for close to two years. I got so spoiled.

The last two days, we had people come up one at a time to see Nina and talk to her. The last day, the last night, was the hardest. She had her best friend, Sammi, and her partner come several times. Before she died, I said, "Honey, how do you want to die? Do you want to die at home? Who do you want around you? Do you want to die here?" She said, "I want to be in my bed with my cats around me. I want to die in your arms, and I want you kissing me." Do you know she stayed alive while I was kissing her? It was about 24 hours of kissing her on the lips. She died with my lips on hers. I felt her take her last breath. People were singing, chanting, soft songs. It was movie worthy.

We have friends that are Catholic from the ashram, and they came, and they wanted to sing the Hail Mary, five rounds of it. I said, "I would rather you make me chew on thorns or something." Swami Jaya Devi came and checked on us, and when Nina died, we bathed her, like the Hindus do. We put oils on her, dressed her, and put flowers all over the bed. It was just so beautiful. Pat and Sharon were here, and Pat made all the arrangements, because that's what she does for a living, and they are my family. Before they cremated her, we had a little viewing for just about 12 of us. She looked so beautiful. And while we were watching her be cremated, down in Florida, they were chanting the Akul, a Hindu prayer where they chant and ring the bells. So, while she was being cremated, we had that happening in Florida as well.

Nina was sick for two years, and it's been five years since she passed. On New Year's Day this year, something hit me with a Rod Stewart song that I love. I listened to it over and over and I just was sobbing. But it was good, and I needed to get it out of my system. It had been so painful to watch her just drifting away from me. After she died, my friends Johnny and Mike stayed around. Pat and my god kids went home. Sharon stayed for three weeks. Thank God for Sharon; she was amazing and loving and was so what I needed and then she had to go home. Johnny brought me coffee every morning up to my bedroom. I just couldn't move. They brought me food and Johnny did all my laundry for two years. Those guys are the best. As Johnny would say, "I loved her more than my underwear." They became like brother and sister. I started feeling like he loved and missed her more than me, which was not true at all. I got spoiled with it. Everybody was around me. I had a lot of people around who wanted to help me. They knew how much I was grieving.

We all were grieving, all our amazing friends and family. I was so angry, but I was also worn out physically, mentally, and emotionally. While Nina was sick, we lost a dear friend, Jerrylin, and then an avalanche of people after she died. I went through a year or two of everybody else dying, my mother, my brother, and I just I was out of it. I worked in my house. I did work and I could maybe see one or two clients, but then I'd have to lay down and sleep. That's how I got through it. I ordered a lot of food through DoorDash and all that. I just wasn't really functioning that well. I stopped exercising. I gained weight. I gained like 30 pounds. Well, then it was Covid. So, I couldn't really do much and I couldn't go out. And I really didn't feel good.

Nina was my soulmate. She was beyond anything I could have hoped for. Everybody still, to this day, says that about her. I was and am still missing all that love, her affection. She was just so affectionate. She would massage my feet, my back; she was just such a caring person. She'd have food on the table when I got home from work. I cooked a lot too, but I never had to worry about a meal. She'd get up and make me my breakfast. I just had all these wonderful things with her. Pat just said the other night about how amazing it was that we met and how Nina was my perfect match to keep me in check. Funny example - when I go to restaurants, God forbid the table isn't situated perfectly! Nina got in the habit of saying before we even went to eat, "Honey, PLEASE be nice and don't critique!" I still laugh about it. Oh well! Ma use to say, "Adita, shut your mouth up."

CHAPTER 15

PUSHING AWAY FROM THE TABLE OF SHAME

Though I was still totally depressed and shaky after Nina's death and so many other losses, I had to make a trip to Philly to spend time with my loved ones. My mom needed to be moved to a new nursing home, my cousin Russ's wife, Mary Pat, was dying and my childhood best friend Josie's mother, who I adored, died. I was a mess driving three to four hours from place to place. Mary Pat was on her death bed, holding on for dear life. She had told me that she wanted to die like Nina did.

So, one night, knowing I had to go back to Josie's house for a dinner party honoring her mother, Mary Pat summoned me to come and trade places with Russ. So, I went over and hold Mary Pat in my arms and the next thing I know she was pointing to her lips to kiss her. When I pulled away, she wanted more. I immediately remembered how I told her I had kissed Nina for over four hours with bits of sleep in between. I wanted to help Mary Pat transition, but with my wife it was a different kind of love devotion. Russ and I were looking at each other amazed. Plus, Mary Pat's sister was sitting right there. So, I was a little embarrassed. Well, I looked at Russ and he had a smile on his face, and I started kissing her. Sweet soft kisses on her lips that lasted for about 20 minutes.

All the while in the back of my mind, I knew I would be late to Josie's. Russ wanted me to sleep there, but I felt such a sense of loyalty to Josie and her family. It was such an awful predicament. Russ and Mary Pat were both crying as I left. I had so many feelings swirling around me. I really should have just gone back to Pat and Sharon's house. I had already called Josie to tell her what was going on. I hadn't been feeling like Josie was understanding all the changes that I had been through in the last 20+ years, and I know that it's hard when your wild and crazy bestie from childhood has grown in a different direction. I then drove an hour to her house. I felt so terrible leaving Mary Pat. Looking back, I know it would have been better if I just stayed at Russ'. It was the last time I saw Mary Pat alive. Since Nina's death and the profound experience of watching the opening and rising of her soul to another dimension and the beauty of it, I have often thought about being a death doula.

It was a hard transition from such a beautiful spiritual space to then having someone who was a little tipsy getting in my face. The minute I walked into Josie's, I got verbally attacked for being late by one of her friends. I knew my reasons and wasn't going to feel guilty. I tried to explain a little and then thought "fuck this." The rest of the group was in the kitchen laughing and having fun. Some people were very nice. As we were gathering around the dining room table, Josie started going off loudly about a good friend who I love, saying some horrible things about her from our youth. She continued after we sat down, trashing her about her previous sex life and how she had turned to God and was now very devout. I was sick of hearing this shit for the last 30 years.

I thought we were going to be sharing stories of her mom. I expected laughter and some celebration of her life. There have been many times I have gotten in trouble making my cousins laugh at funerals. And I am still guilty of gossip and Josie was used to me being that way. We could laugh all night long about people and things. It was what she was saying about this person in the most demeaning way. I couldn't handle it. I still get sick in my stomach when I think about it and her kids who had never met this person were there listening in. I just think Josie had always been jealous of her because from the minute that person and I met in high school, we became best buds.

There was so much shame and blame being thrown around. It was like a group of teenagers, talking trash about friends under the guise of humor. I had been experiencing some separation over the years from Josie, starting back to when I came out to her, and I knew if I discussed our differences, she would fly off the handle. We had always been close; I was Godmother to her two children. I couldn't tell her anything about the growth and change, which had been ongoing in my life for many years, because she really didn't understand. While I appreciated that her husband was a good father and provider, I never really liked him. He was homophobic and Josie kept my dating women from him for 30 years, until I met Nina. His views contributed to our distance. I'm not going to air our dirty laundry out here, but what I used to think of as funny as a teenager simply wasn't funny at all. After hearing so many unkind things, I didn't want any part of that. I thank God for my recovery. All my growth brought into focus that this was another relationship that was disintegrating, and I didn't want it to be. I had been trying to hold on for a very long time.

Shame and Dignity

I had to fight hard to let go of the shame I was raised with. My grandfather and the demeaning way he spoke to me and my siblings and used very foul language in front of us eroded our dignity. Although I praise my Grandfather Lou to the high Heavens, he did a lot of damage and so did several others. He was so critical of my mom and my dad, rightfully so, and I took all that in as my own shame. They made it okay to talk horribly about others right in front of them or behind their backs. That was not okay, and I did that too until I learned better. Shame erodes dignity and self-worth.

Many of my family members passed shame around the table, whether it was in a soft voice (never) or a loud voice (always). I was shamed on a regular basis about my weight and as a teenager about my changing body. Unless I looked like a mamadelle (opposite of sexy), my grandfather Lou would go off the deep end. Now, when I am anywhere where shame is passed around the table, I leave.

Shame is one of the hardest things to get rid for many reasons. Addicts have been taught shame from when they are little. Victims of sexual assault carry shame. It is very pervasive, and you start feeling that your very essence is shame that you are shame itself rather than just an action you took. There are many books to help deal with this topic. I have done a lot of work on shame in my 12-step programs, at the ashram, and I listen to tapes from weekend workshops that Ma did particularly on shame. Shame is a thing that is hard to break through. But being with them, I clearly saw it all around the table. I do not want to be in those environments anymore.

In my family, they didn't care who they did it in front of. My grandfather shamed my mother one time when she had a date. He didn't care who he shamed her in front of, and she could never bring a man home. I have done so much shame work. It's hard to break. This behavior at that funeral was a clear picture of what I used to endure.

Depending on what spiritual or religious background you are born into, almost everyone believes that just by being born into a body and being human we possess dignity. We come into this world with it. We have intrinsic value. Some of the ways we develop dignity is through how we are treated and how we see other people treated. We all need love and compassion. I personally lost a lot of my compassion, probably more like buried it, for years. From the time I got hollered at for crying or not being allowed to express my feelings, I didn't know the words to describe what was going on. Being told to act dignified was a stark contrast to how I felt inside and how I was treated at home. How could I really feel dignified and claim my dignity if I feared that my father was going to rape me, and when he said the meanest things, or when constantly getting hit or hollered at and punished because I was overweight?

I watched my grandmother and mother being cursed at and my mother being called a whore when she wasn't at all. My grandfather Lou's mouth was over the top a lot of the time and not dignified in any way, especially when he was drinking. I didn't feel valued at home except when I made my Grandfather Lou happy by eating with him or making other people laugh. I was very lucky to have my Grandparents Sue and Tony who instilled in me that I was worthy every chance they had to compliment me. I had to fight hard to reclaim all that, especially after the beatings from Paul and the way he spoke to me. It thrust me into awareness of who I was and how I wanted to be. I will always be an advocate for children, women, and people who were or are abused and don't realize the extent that it plays out on them and others.

Again, if I haven't said it before, I'll say it now. My grandfather Lou had lots of problems. He had a nervous breakdown and had shock treatments before I was born. I'm not sure what caused that, but I suspect it was his own trauma growing up. His uncles "playfully" tortured him in Italy, hanging him on a tree over some water and then he and his mother missed out on two boats to America before finally securing room on a third. When they reunited with his father in America, he endured his father beating his mother, sometimes even in the streets, as a little boy. So, from generation to generation, experiencing all that shame and loss of self, any sense of dignity and self-respect flew out the window.

My Mothers Death and Making Peace with Jesus

I was always at odds with my mom from the time I was in her womb, but we were also like best friends. Maybe she wasn't the mom I wanted, but we went to hair shows together. We went out to eat together. My ex and I took her to the shore with Josie's mother. We spent a lot of our lives together. She went to work every day. She loved going out. She would say, "Let's go to New York. Let's go to the casino." Because we were so close in age, Mom was more like a friend and wanted to go everywhere with me.

Mom loved fine things even when she was older. When I would visit, she would ask, "Where'd you get that jewelry?" My wife went to visit her once and she was wearing a fur vest and jacket. My mother asked her, "Oh my god, where'd you get that jacket?" She did have Alzheimer's, but it was more like some very deep state of depression. She was depressed her whole life and lived in a fantasy world most of the time. The real world was just too painful for her.

My mother spent the last ten years of her life in the nursing home. *Who lasts that long?* I had noticed her mental decline for about two years. Before we moved her to the nursing home, she still lived in the house we grew up in after my grandparents passed. My brother Louis lived with her. I would go home at least three or four times a year, and my cousins would come over to visit. I loved it because it gave me an excuse to go to my favorite Italian places and get freshly made mozzarella, cherry peppers stuffed with extra sharp cheese and prosciutto, all kinds of wonderful sandwiches stuffed with fried cutlets and broccoli rappini, and cannoli.

It was so great having my family together, and then I started noticing oddities like the sugar bowl in the refrigerator. I asked my cousin Linda if Mom seemed a little off one day, and she replied, "Not any more than usual." I laughed. When I questioned mom, she showed her typical sarcastic annoyance with me. She was still walking to the Italian market, to church, and was still able to pay her bills. But Mom had been losing her closest family one by one. When her sister, my aunt Marian died, I think that did her in. Even through all the loss, Mom couldn't cry. Me, on the other hand, threw myself on top of my grandmother in the hospital room bed when she died. I was sobbing uncontrollably.

My mother couldn't go out anymore so my brother had to keep her in, and she would just scream. Eventually, he and my sister got her into a nursing home. See? They could do things without me. Mom adapted quite well. My mom had always been so racist, and I really think she was just scared because of all the segregation and race riots in Philly back in the day. But I had to laugh because the place was about 75 percent Black, and Mom grew to love her roommate, Eunice. They became inseparable, walking around holding hands and always eating together. The biggest joy for me was that she was Black. I loved that at times she thought Eunice was me or one her sisters. I hope my aunts saw that from heaven! Eventually, Covid hit, and Eunice passed, and it broke our hearts. We loved her and she would do and say the funniest things and kept Mom laughing. I sure hope I get to see Eunice again in the afterlife. My mom became friends with another petite, dark-skinned woman who was also lovely and they became friends and were always giggling, too.

My sister thought they were not taking good care of Mom, so we decided to move her to a nicer place. The minute we pulled up, I knew my mom wasn't gonna last there. It was a lot of smoke and mirrors. My intuition when we brought her there, though it was a very nice place, I got a zing that said, *this is where your mother's going to die.* The other place was paid for by the state, but while this one was not, it was more upscale. She was at that other one for nine years. The women there loved her because she'd advise them on their hair, their makeup, and everything. She loved their jewelry.

Most of the population there were dressed nicely, and at the events, most of them were in wheelchairs and I could see their eyes were very glazed over. I realized they were over-medicating them to keep them docile. While the main person was doing the intake for Mom, I saw right through her. I even said to her, "You're so slick, you could work on Wall Street." She looked at me with her glasses on the tip of her nose and she said, "I'm sure you could, too."

My mom died about six months later. None of the physical therapy she was supposed to get ever happened. She couldn't walk so she got pneumonia and that was that. One of the things that blew me away was all the empathy I was feeling for my mom. Even though I had been worshipping in the Hindu tradition, while I was with mom, I called for the priest to give her the last rites. I am so proud I did that for her, and it turned out to be a real blessing to me to see it done. There is a part of it that is called the Apostolic Pardon that is optional. As the priest was doing this prayer, I saw my mother's face totally change, and it was more beautiful than ever. All the stress and all the guilt she carried all those years just vanished into thin air.

I had to come back to Atlanta as Mom was lingering. My siblings and cousin, Johnny Maratea, went to be by her side. Mom died in her sleep. I always thought that her death wouldn't bother me that much because I had been grieving her as she declined in the nursing home. I always worried about Mom and fantasized that Uncle Fred and Aunt Connie would come to her rescue if she needed anything. When my grandmother died, they were keeping a big secret about the will. All the while, the will was written so that my mom could live in her childhood home until she died. I still wish my uncle would've told me that my grandmother had ensured that Mom's needs would be taken care of, because he knew how much I worried about her. My brother Louis lived there until he died.

I took a big hit after Mom died. She was also the tenth person I lost in the four years following Nina's death. Then, my brother died and my cousin Sammy who I adored. Everyone kept saying they didn't know how I was handling this. I didn't know either.

My spiritual practice, teaching yoga, and meditation helped soothe me, but it wasn't enough. I gained 50 pounds during Nina's illness and her death. I had lost 25 of them before my mom died. I started to put weight back on, and I stopped exercising. During all the years of my food addiction, through the gaining and losing, the one thing I had never done was force myself to throw up. And now, I started purging because I was binging and couldn't even breathe. I didn't want to tell anyone, not even my sponsor or my therapist. It really got bad, and I couldn't control it. I prayed to God. I prayed to Baba, Ma's guru. Nothing was working.

I was at the Florida ashram which had always been a lifesaver for me. There was a beautiful event going on with lots of prayers, chanting, and a big fire puja in which we threw rice in to get rid of our character defects. The event was all in front of the big Baba Temple. Many of my friends had been telling me for 20 years to pray to Baba about my addictions. Maybe Baba has been helping me, but to be honest, I just never felt anything from Baba. Many of the Hindu saints I felt helped me to work through my karma and issues to bring me to who I am today.

That weekend I was begging Baba to help me, and I just wasn't feeling anything. I was questioning it because so many hundreds, maybe thousands, of addicts got clean from being Ma and Baba devotees. In the 1950s, people started flocking to India to study with Maharishi and get clean. That still thrives today. None of that was helping me. I was vomiting and gaining weight. I just couldn't comprehend losing my mother. I was always so angry with her passivity and dependence on her family. While she was in the nursing home, I had a hard time talking to her on the phone, but as much as she always annoyed me, I missed talking about all the food, fashion, and music, and gossiping. I bought her really cool stuff while she was in the hospital and even until the end, she remained a fashionista and wanted anything that my sister and I, and even Nina, had on that was high-fashion.

Mom being gone was way more than I could handle and I was distraught. So, after pleading with Baba, I was able to go up to Ma's private rooms and pray. Just walking through Kashi House where Ma lived brought on an instant, wonderful amount of spiritual energy on high. I knelt before Ma's bed that she died in and where we all went up to see her. I knelt at the foot of her bed and was just sobbing and told her how Baba never worked for me and to please help me with my relationship with Baba. Another teacher, who I followed and know, had lived with Baba in India and always said that Baba had Christ energy.

After sobbing for a while, I got up and sat in the big leather chair facing Ma's bed, doing some breath work to try to calm down and then suddenly it felt as if everywhere in the rooms it got darker, and I was twisting and turning. Suddenly, I felt I was at my Grandmother Suzy Q's house where she would constantly remind me about Jesus. And the way I turned, I noticed the statute of the Pieta with Mary holding Jesus after He came off the cross. My grandmothers always loved it, but I never felt a connection to it. Perhaps because I had already experienced a lot of grief and sadness and didn't think I had room for anymore.

But in that moment, I was overwhelmed by compassion for Mary and Jesus. I had connected to all the agony I went through trying to save my wife. I felt Jesus' presence in the room, and I heard Jesus say to me, "You can't have a relationship with Baba until you come through Me." I was stunned. I resonated with the fierceness of the Hindu Goddess Kali. And now I was feeling a flood of compassion, empathy, and love for Jesus, finally remembering my Catholic school teachings. I stayed on the chair a while in amazement and sat with my newfound feelings of love, peace, and joy. From this point forward, many things have shifted for me.

I came home blissed out and thinking of all the teachings of Christ that now made sense to me. I never totally gave up on Christ, but I was just always pissed off at the Catholic Church for as long as I could remember for all the guilt and shame pushed on us. I now felt relieved with a newfound freedom. But I joke about it and say, "I made up with Christ." I had been angry with Him since I was eight, and now, I felt such a sense of calm.

By the time I came home to Atlanta, I was saturated with bliss. And before I knew it, the vomiting stopped. Actually, it had started to get better while I was at the ashram. When I returned a few months later, I couldn't wait to go up to Ma's rooms. It is my favorite place to be. I was really stoked that Jesus would maybe talk to me again and guide me. I did my same routine. I walked into Ma's rooms bowing with my hands in prayer to all the statues and kneeling at the foot of Ma's bed in full Pranam. Since recovery, I immediately move forward with my gratitude list to God! I was thanking God and then I heard Jesus saying, "You need to learn how to forgive." And I got it. Oh well, I've been working on this for years and so the Man upstairs is finally telling me what I need to do.

Unending Loss

The same month Nina died, two of my best male buddies, Dick and Russell, died. They were people that I would go out with every Friday night. Jim, the dearest of all, died shortly after. And my friend Jerrylin died two months before Nina, followed by my cousin Mary Pat. And then my cousin Sammy who was so special to me died. It just went on and on. Three of my favorite Swamis died. These were people who along the way were bearers of my growth and truth. It all was very painful.

And then came the drama of my brother's death, who died from a heart attack. I loved him so much. But when he died, people made up a whole bunch of lies about him being murdered and that he was shot. It was crazy. It triggered some of my PTSD. None of it was true. I talked to my brother through my medium. I called Rosie next door. I was hysterical. I couldn't find my sister Sadie.

She was even telling people in the neighborhood that he got killed and it wasn't true. You would have thought that my brother might have died that way because of some of the things he had done, but that wasn't it. He had a friend come over to help him fix the air conditioner. He was very depressed over our mom dying. He was with my mom for 30 years. He was 60 something, and he still lived at home.

I don't think he could deal with it, so a friend came over to help him fix the air conditioner in the window, and they couldn't get it fixed. So, he took it out and laid it on the floor. They blamed it on this kid that was a former drug addict that used to go over to the house and help him fix things. I was so frustrated with all the different crazy stories I was being told. Finally, I said, "I know who I'm going to call. I'm going to call Greg, my medium." And right away the message came through. My brother said, "I wasn't killed. The kid was there to help me with the air conditioner. We couldn't get it fixed it. I put it on the floor, and it was very heavy, but the reason I died was my heart gave out".

Louis had a rod put up his back from when he fell down the subway steps. They wanted to put a new rod up there, but he was too afraid of something going wrong and ending up in a wheelchair and so he was taking pain medicine. He said that his back was hurting. They found him at the kitchen table near his medicines. He didn't have drugs in his body. So, it seems that he just had a heart attack. They took his body to do an autopsy. The detective who was working the case told me that he had no bruises. There was no blood in the house or on him. He said there were no signs of forced entry. All the doors were locked. The back screen door was unlocked, but that was it. Crazy people were going around saying he was murdered. He was not. They were still floating unnecessary drama around the streets. This is what I had to deal with my whole life. Crazy shit from day one.

I kept thinking about how much I loved Louis when my mom brought him home from the hospital as a sweet, chubby baby. I would take him places with me as I did Sadie. I saw what was happening, and I always tried to be a mom to them. He started drugs very young, and I always felt like I lost my brother when that happened. He had so many advantages and opportunities that he couldn't seem to hold onto, including a scholarship to the art institute and holding a Union position. But Louis' life was controlled by drugs, and he spent years doing nothing. He had created a beautiful space to do his art in the basement. Dad probably secured Louis' demise when he tried to pressure him into selling drugs for him. Louis was not my father; he wasn't as smart or as vicious and his addiction kept him at a continual disadvantage. While he was able to sell some of his beautiful paintings, he had such untapped creative potential and seeing the vestiges of his addiction and choices were horrifying. Everyone in the family tried to help him, but as I see it, they didn't understand addictions or how 12-step programs save thousands of lives. He was partly ruined by our family who raised him and those around us. I also think a lot of people in our family were afraid of him because he would get violent. There were times he would start hitting me, and I had to run next door to Uncle Joe's house. I was feeling all the pain and sorrow for what was and is lost.

After four years of constant loss, I felt so alone—no wife, mom gone, brother gone, sister distraught. In my neighborhood growing up, there was no difference between first, second, and third cousins. They were like siblings. There was always a cousin to hang out with. I saw them every day until I left Philly.

Leaving Philly had been traumatic for me. I didn't realize it at first because Lynn and I were traveling constantly. We lived in a great neighborhood and had this big, beautiful home and great neighbors that are now dear friends. I was also doing great in the salon and doing better than ever financially. Lynn and I had broken up, and I never moved to Los Angeles. I was always missing that sense of having my family around me. I have built an incredible community in Atlanta. When I met Nina and she moved here, it helped fill the longing I felt for Philly and my family in some ways. Nina also made so many friends here and everyone just loved her. We did all the Italian traditions that we both knew and loved.

Since Nina died, I am again feeling that loss around Philly. I know Philly isn't anything like it used to be, and my family and the old neighborhood have dispersed. Nina represented what I loved most about Philly and my family. I have never stopped missing those things. I also have a great diverse community where I live and have made lots of good friends and neighbors.

When Nina died, I was so despondent, and a friend of mine was very worried about me. I worked and stayed busy on Saturdays, but Sundays were the worst. On Sundays, I would just want to bury myself under the bed, because that was always the day Nina and I spent time together or in quiet reflection. I was distraught and so, one day, my friend said, "I think it would be good for you to teach." You know how they talk about service is so good? I started teaching a group breathwork, yoga, and meditation, which went on for about three years. I recently stopped teaching because I wanted to take the time to write my story.

I was also healed by an artist and spiritual teacher named Krishna Das. His music, which is folk Hindu music always transforms my soul and mood, and it sends me into outer space. He carries a certain vibration in his voice that heals.

There were friends who came in for breakfast, lunch, and either brought me dinner or invited me over. That's what saved my life because I felt like I wanted to die after Nina was gone. I never had anybody like her in all my years. My friends knew what I liked and what I missed and filled me up with so much love.

I also found solace in the music of k.d. lang. I went through pictures of Nina when she was young and found several where she and k.d. looked very similar. I sent two pictures of Nina to k.d. on Twitter, including one of Nina in the outfit she wore to our wedding, and they thought it was k.d. They kept one of Nina's pictures in k.d. lang's online portfolio. I always loved her music, and I have seen her several times in person. What pisses me off is that I was in LA quite often and Lynn and I went out to clubs dancing, while nearby k.d. was hanging out in a different club with Ellen DeGeneres and all the gorgeous people. I know I would have been trying to get my butt in there to meet k.d. had I known she was so close, but I was so in love with Lynn at that time that it didn't faze me. She can be very kind, seems so authentic, and I love that she is a Buddhist. After Nina's death, k.d. lang and her music, honest to God, soothed me. The other things that got me through my grief were my art, my spiritual life, music, friends and family, and teaching yoga and meditation.

Diva Adita

I could never really say I am or was a princess, and yet, I totally love when I'm treated like one, providing there are no expectations. I have worked hard all my life to get what I wanted and needed. And, yes, I love things to be beautiful and elegant. When I was little, Susie Q would take me to the beach and would bring along little plastic bags that held washcloths to wipe me down at the top of the boardwalk. When I reached a certain age, she would let me sit in the front seat of the car with my grandfather. That's how bad she wanted me to drive, to be independent. My Aunt Connie's house was beautiful and elegant. Their parties were special and refined. When I would go see my mom work at Wanamaker's, her friends would want to give me facials. Dad taught me about fine dining, and his aesthetics in everything he did showed me a certain level of sophistication. And Mom was beautiful and made everything look pretty. I was prepared for the proper way to behave at very nice establishments.

Working at the Bellevue and the Ritz Carlton in Atlanta and learning about service there continued my education in the finer things in life. My customers at the Ritz were amazing. When I would travel for shows, I would get the royal treatment. One time, in Laguna Niguel, they set me up on the fifth or sixth floor so I could watch the skydivers and the people in floating balloons right over the Pacific. They would send up a great bottle of wine for me at events and it was fabulous.

Even our set up for our clients was beautiful. We had an airline attendant working as a hostess at the Bellevue serving complimentary beverages and snacks at both Jamison Shaw Salon and Who's Who. At the Ritz, we had a soda machine and all kinds of great snacks. Several famous chefs were my clients. They would send down desserts or once there was a blind tasting to find something more affordable than Cristal champagne. I reveled in this, and the best part was that I really appreciated being a part of it all. The hard work that I had been doing for years was taking hold so that my insides were matching my outsides.

At the Ashram, I often stayed with friends. My friends', Ronnie and Gail's, house looked like a small Los Angeles movie director's house. It's on two lots with a swimming pool and has gorgeous landscaping. Not too long ago, I was staying in one of the newer rooms of the Ashram in Florida that was decorated beautifully with a nice, plush queen bed, a leather couch, and a mini kitchen with a little coffee pot. When I went to make the coffee, it was from Publix. They used to have Dancing Goats, which is from here in Atlanta. And now I had to drink Publix coffee. A friend came over and I was complaining, "Can you believe this fucking coffee? It's horrible! I drink espresso every day at home." The answer from her was, "Listen, Italian Princess Adita, remember you are at an Ashram, not the Ritz Carlton." We both cracked up. I had stayed at her beautiful home, and she would get crazy over all my luggage. Who wouldn't? But I did have my Nespresso machine and frother! And it wasn't like she didn't have a whole set up of Keurig coffee and all the accoutrements!

Even Ma treated me like a diva. When I would arrive, she would shout, "My Adita is here!" It irritated some people, probably the Atlantans. But some would say, "Adita, when you come here, Ma acts like a movie star has arrived." A young lady who grew up on the Ashram said, "Adita, even when Ma is killing you (meaning working to rid you of your ego), it's like she's making love to you." I would laugh. I knew Ma and a lot of the Florida people loved when I arrived for many different reasons. I miss Ma and those days so much!

So, I guess I have gotten used to very nice things and wonderful people. Every day, I am so glad to be blessed like this and several times a day I say how grateful I am. I have worked very hard to get to this place.

Resilience and Positivity

People have told me that I'm actually the hero of my own story. Maybe that's due to a lifetime of resilience and positivity. I decided from the beginning that I'm going to find a way to do what I want to do with my life and not hold back.

Even with all the "nos" I received as a child, I somehow pushed through them. At the Mallace house, my grandmother was always hollering at me for wasting paper and pencils. Her hollering was very soft compared to any other Italian voice I knew. Once, I was punished for who knows what and I went down to the basement to listen to my albums. I hated those cement walls. There was an album out at the time called *Up Against the Wall Mother Fucker* and on the cover were cops frisking guys with their hands up against a graffiti-covered wall. I loved that vibe and look. *Oh well, you assholes punished me again so I'll day glow paint the walls with graffitti.* It was so neon bright that my uncle couldn't paint over it.

At that point in life, I was developing my resilience. One of my aunts told me about a book by Dr. Burns, *Feeling Good: The New Mood Therapy,* and I start reading it. When I first went to therapy, that was the model they were working with. My attitude started changing and my life changed with it. None of this was easy. I was sick of everybody and everything. Because I had built up such resilience when I started applying positivity to the situations, things really started to change. I didn't know these intersections before; I just kept on doing the next best thing. It may have been easier if Paul was out of the picture, but I just let my empathy combined with fear overrule me.

Whether it was gaining weight, losing weight, losing partners, dealing with an abusive man, or dealing with losing the woman I loved, I prayed to God to help me walk through it with a positive attitude and grace. *How am I going to be positive today? How can I walk away and move to the next thing and the next thing despite my stumbling blocks?* Many years ago, when I was told by an Indian master that I could not do a yoga pose because my body was not right for that, it was painful and derailed me. But I ultimately proved him wrong, finding my way back to Yoga and even taking a Yoga teachers course. I'm pretty sure this is where reading *Gone with the Wind* four times that summer, I was punished left a lasting impression. Scarlett was tenacious. It was a soothing balm for all the choked back tears I held in all the previous years. I remember so many times I had to scream and punch into the pillow so my grandfather or my mother wouldn't hear me. I believe that's when I learned more about resilience. You must have resilience to survive this world. I saw all the immigrants hustling and bustling around me. They had resilience and determination.

EPILOGUE

G rowing up, I got so used to being a victim and surviving all the chaos around me that I continued to put myself in similar situations over and over again, waiting for someone to save me. I don't know about you, but I have done that many times and then I bitch about it. There was so much drama in my world that I grew up thinking it was all normal. When you fear your parents and family members as a young child and they scream at you in front of other people, you begin to lose your dignity. So, by the time Paul came along, even in the beginning, I knew he was violent, but it was familiar. Through all of this, I was always trying to better myself and learn everything I could. I knew that would be key to escaping my Italian prison. Yet, I loved my culture and my big Italian family and didn't want to give that up, nor did I have to.

My life was very complicated and filled with contradictions. Even though I had this criminal dad, I loved him, and he taught me so many interesting things. Some of his brilliance always amazed me and I admired those qualities in him. He recognized my interests and encouraged them by taking me to art museums and places to inspire me. This is where I believe my natural brilliance and aptitude comes in. Thankfully, early on, I was able to recognize and see the best and worst in every family member. Even as a very young girl, I saw this and spent a lot of time around the people who I wanted to emulate, especially my mom's sisters who I loved and admired. I incorporated the parts of them that I admired, and later in life, worked to get rid of any of the negatives that I had unconsciously adopted.

Spiritual practices have changed me and the connections I have with people on Earth and even after death. I work hard to keep the channels open. It has been extremely difficult for me to accept that I hated and loved my dad at the same time, or any of the so called "mobsters" that I knew. It was hard to understand how someone like Tony Soprano came home after killing someone and loved his family.

There was a time my dad was unexpectantly at my grandmother's, and I was happy to see him. He was on the phone with his back to me as I came in. I was excited to see him, and I went behind him and hollered, "Hey, Dad." He turned around with the phone held in his hand like he was going to kill me with it. It was the scariest look I ever saw on his face. Somehow, after he realized it was me and how happy I was to see him, he softened. I immediately saw killer instincts in his face or maybe it was from prison when he was on the phone and there were always people in line waiting to use the phone. But in that moment, I knew my dad was a killer. I surmised it all along. It shook my whole world after that.

The Marty Hess murder affected my whole life. It took so much to get rid of the fear, shame, and guilt. And feeling like I could've done something to prevent his murder. How could I? When the very cops who were supposed to be protecting him were the cops who did the crime. They got indicted and went to jail. Even after I moved away, four decades after the murder, every now and again, I get fearful as I put the key in the car ignition. Will this be the time the I get blown to bits in some unknown act of revenge? That feeling was so strong from 1972-2015. A sponsor helped me realize how deep my fears ran, and I did several types of therapy to get rid of the PTSD.

It was hard to love and have compassion for myself and recognize my self-worth. I found love not just in others, but in myself. I learned that one way to increase my self-worth is by doing estimable acts. Extending myself to others through service has been instrumental to my growth and filled me with love and empathy.

We all have inherent value and deserve dignity, love, respect, and happiness, regardless of our circumstances. I did not learn this as a child, especially coming from a 16-year-old mother and 17-year-old juvenile delinquent father. It sure has been painful, and yet, I am beyond grateful to have found myself. If my story can help one or a thousand to offer them a life of peace, self-worth, joy, and love, I will know my journey is not for naught. My younger self didn't always know the words to describe what I was feeling, and I was not comfortable with how my grandfather talked to my mom, my grandmother, or me.

I knew something had to change. I wanted more dignity and respect, not only for me, but for my mother, grandmother, and siblings. All this hard work has given me a level of peace, love, and self-respect that I had no idea existed. I have intimacy with self, and I love it. Those times when I was screaming into the pillow sobbing and thinking about Scarlett O'Hara's strength, I realized something very important. I was learning about resilience, strength, and solidarity of self. I knew I was gonna be like her and that's what I wanted. I recognized and modeled that through the years. If you can stand in solidarity with self, you will then also know the true value of solidarity with others.

I chose my own role in life. I chose me. My life didn't turn because of luck; it turned because I fought for it. Maybe that's due to a lifetime of developing resiliency and positivity. Words and sayings come to me at different times, and I search to fully understand how they apply. This has happened to me for many years. I have learned to look at it and if it's good, to marinate in it; and if it's negative, let it go. In either case, I learned the importance of morning pages and journaling. Answers always come. I have found that when I am grounded in self-love, I am much more loving to others and the frailties of the human condition.

It is very important for me to be around people and friends who support each other. I seek out people who believe in me. I love to share and support others as well. I still just love to hang out, to laugh, and talk shit. I opt to be around people who are positive and speak kindly. That was not always the case. I am just as guilty as anyone for not always saying the nicest things. My job is to make amends as soon as I can. I must say that I have some of the smartest, loving friends and customers in the world. As I deepen my spiritual practices, it has changed me and my connectedness to the Divine. I really work hard to keep the channels open. Being in that Divine Flow is not always easy while living in this world. So many things have helped me in changing my life. For me, yoga, meditation, and journaling are at the top of my list.

All the words that pop up in my head when I awaken like self-solidarity, dignity, resiliency, and positivity are connected. I realized now how each of these intersect and how we need each one to live a full beautiful life. Writing about them has taught me how amazing the connections are between them all. Last thought…they say book writing is cathartic; it sure is. Hold that thought. My next book on how I lost 160 pounds and how I have kept it for off for 40 years is in the works! I was not born to be quiet, obedient, or forgettable.

ACKNOWLEDGEMENTS

Thanks to all my teachers, mentors, aunts and uncles who were there along the way. And to my grandparents for giving me and my siblings a strong foundation. It really does take a village.

To all my cousins—first, second, third and even fourth—that surrounded me with love and laughter, and still do. I don't know how I would've made it without you. We all know we have each other's backs.

Thank you to my friends who have become family—Pat, Sharon, Danny and Sophie and Johnny and Mike.

With gratitude to my neighbors and friends in Philly and Atlanta, especially those who saw me through so much loss and grief and those who were instrumental in the genesis of this book.

To all the salon owners and amazing hair artists who I worked with for taking my craft to the top, opening doors for me and providing business advice.

To our interfaith ashram for providing the choice to worship in ways that resonated with me and to the Swamis for their dedication to the service of mankind.

To Jerry Davis, my first writing coach who put me on the path of The Artist's Way.

And to Lil Barcaski my publisher for her perseverance.

Special thanks to Dr. Rick Kilmore for all his wisdom, guidance and grace.

And to the Al-Anon program for saving my life and changing it forever.

And to Olive, the best/worst writing assistant that salmon treats could buy and her good friend, Monica.

Elaine Adita Agnes is an author, speaker, and spiritual teacher known for her multifaceted life as a fashionista hairstylist, makeup artist, and proud lesbian living life out loud. Raised in a chaotic, mob-connected Italian family in South Philly, Adita draws from her personal journey of reinvention and resilience, fueled by meditation and yoga, to share funny and unfiltered wisdom from Atlanta, Georgia.

www.ingramcontent.com/pod-product-compliance
Lightning Source LLC
Chambersburg PA
CBHW061729120626
46550CB00005B/1753